A SIMPLE PATH

Selected books by His Holiness the Dalai Lama
published by Thorsons

Transforming the Mind
The Power of Compassion
The Art of Living

A SIMPLE PATH

BASIC BUDDHIST TEACHINGS BY HIS HOLINESS THE DALAI LAMA

Translated by Geshe Thupten Jinpa
Edited by Dominique Side

Photographs by Ian Cumming

Thorsons

Thorsons
An Imprint of HarperCollins*Publishers*
77-85 Fulham Palace Road,
Hammersmith, London W6 8JB

The Thorsons website address is: www.thorsons.com

and *Thorsons* are trademarks of
HarperCollins*Publishers* Ltd

First published as *The Four Noble Truths*
This edition published by Thorsons 2002

3 5 7 9 10 8 6 4 2

A catalogue record of this book is
available from the British Library

HB ISBN 0 00 710550 9
PB ISBN 0 00 713887 3

Printed and bound in Hong Kong

CONTENTS

Preface 6

INTRODUCTION 8

THE FOUR NOBLE TRUTHS 22

THE TRUTH OF SUFFERING 36

THE TRUTH OF THE ORIGIN OF SUFFERING 82

THE TRUTH OF CESSATION 116

THE TRUTH OF THE PATH 148

Glossary 170   Notes 173

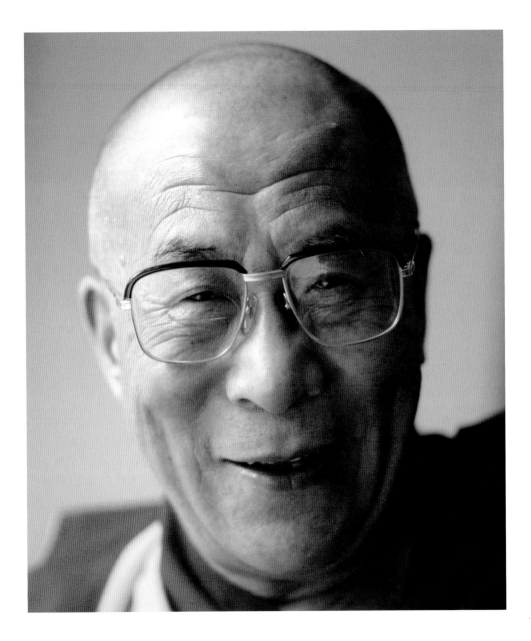

PREFACE

The text of *A Simple Path* is based upon teachings given by His Holiness the Dalai Lama in London in 1996. The theme of the teachings and the book is the Four Noble Truths, which is the foundation of all Buddha's teachings. In these pages, His Holiness presents a comprehensive explanation of the subject. Published previously in volume form with other lectures, His Holiness's teachings on the Four Noble Truths have been edited and presented here in a new context, complete with photographs to help the reader appreciate the rich cultural heritage of Tibetan Buddhism. Photographer Ian Cumming's images of landscapes and Tibetan people, both the monastic community and lay Buddhist practitioners, help to deepen an awareness of the context in which Tibetan Buddhism developed and is now being preserved in exile. Rather than attempting to illustrate the words of His Holiness, the images provide a loose accompaniment to the text. For example, an image of a pilgrim prostrating before the Potala Palace, the former home of the Dalai Lama, helps to convey the preciousness with which these teachings and Tibet's spiritual leader are held.

The Office of Tibet in London would like to thank Cait Collins and Jane Rasch for transcribing the tapes of the talks, and Dominique Side and the translator Geshe Thupten Jinpa for editing the manuscript for publication.

INTRODUCTION

THE FOUR NOBLE TRUTHS ARE
THE VERY FOUNDATION OF THE
BUDDHIST TEACHING

The Four Noble Truths are the very foundation of the Buddhist teaching. In fact, if you don't understand the Four Noble Truths, and if you have not experienced the truth of this teaching personally, it is impossible to practice Buddha Dharma. Therefore I am always very happy to have the opportunity to explain them.

Generally speaking, I believe that all the major world religions have the potential to serve humanity and develop good human beings. By "good" I mean that they have a good and more compassionate heart. This is why I always say it is better to follow one's own traditional religion, because by changing religion you may eventually find emotional or intellectual difficulties.

However, for those of you who really feel that your traditional religion is not effective for you then the Buddhist way of explaining things may hold some attraction. Maybe in this case it is all right to follow Buddhism generally, I think it is better to have some kind of religious training than none at all. If you really feel attracted to the Buddhist approach, and the Buddhist way of training the mind, it is important to reflect carefully, and only when you feel it is really suitable for you is it right to adopt Buddhism as your religion.

There is another important point here. Human nature is such that sometimes, in order to justify our adoption of a new religion, we may criticize our previous religion and claim it is inadequate. This should not happen. Firstly, although your previous religion may not be effective for you, that does not mean it will fail to be of value to millions of other people. Since we should respect all human beings, we must also respect those following different religious paths. It is clear that for some people the Christian approach is more effective than the Buddhist one. It depends on the individual's mental disposition. We must therefore appreciate that potential in each religion, and respect all those who follow them.

The second reason is that we are now becoming aware of the many religious traditions of the world, and people are trying to promote genuine harmony between them. I think there are now many interfaith circles and the idea of religious pluralism is taking root. This is a very encouraging sign.

I wanted to begin with these points, because when I actually explain the Four Noble Truths, I have to argue the Buddhist way is the best! Also, if you were to ask me what the best religion is for me personally, my answer would be Buddhism, without any hesitation. But that does not mean that Buddhism is best for everyone – certainly not. Therefore, during the course of my explanation, when I say that I feel that the Buddhist way is best, you should not misunderstand me.

I would like to further emphasize that when I say that all religions have great potential, I am not just being polite or diplomatic. I have met genuine practitioners from other traditions. I have noticed a genuine and very forceful loving kindness in their minds. My conclusion therefore is that these various religions have the potential to develop a good heart.

Whether or not we like the philosophy of other religions isn't really the point. For a non-Buddhist, the idea of nirvana and a next life seems nonsensical. Similarly, to Buddhists the idea of a Creator God sometimes sounds like nonsense. But these things don't matter; we can drop them. The point is that through these different traditions, a very negative person can be transformed into a good person. That is the purpose of religion – and that is the actual result. This alone is a sufficient reason to respect other religions.

There is one last point. As you may know, Buddha taught in different ways, and Buddhism has a variety of philosophical systems. If the Buddha taught in these different ways, it would seem that he himself was not very sure about how things really are! But this is not actually the case; the Buddha knew the different mental dispositions of his followers. So even Buddha Shakyamuni very much respected the views and rights of individuals. A teaching may be very profound but if it does not suit a particular person, what is the use of explaining it?

BASIC PRINCIPLES OF BUDDHISM

Whenever I introduce the Buddhist teachings, I make a point of presenting them in terms of two basic principles. The first of these is the interdependent nature of reality.[1] All Buddhist philosophy rests on an understanding of this basic truth. The second principle is non-violence, which is the action taken by a Buddhist practitioner who has the view of the interdependent nature of reality. Non-violence essentially means that we should do our best to help others and, if this is not possible, should at the very least refrain from harming them. Before I explain the Four Noble Truths in detail, I propose to outline both these principles by way of background.

TAKING REFUGE AND GENERATING BODHICHITTA

First, I will introduce these principles in traditional Buddhist terms. Technically, we become a Buddhist when we decide to take Refuge in the Three Jewels, and when we generate bodhichitta, which is known as compassion, the altruistic mind, or our good heart. The Three Jewels of Buddhism are the Buddha; the Dharma, his teaching; and the Sangha or community of practitioners. It is very clear that the idea of helping others lies at the heart of both Refuge and Bodhichitta. The practice of Generating Bodhichitta explicitly entails committing oneself to activities which are primarily aimed at helping others; while the practice of Taking Refuge lays the foundation for the practitioner to lead his or her life in an ethically disciplined way.

Unless we have a good foundational experience of the practice of Taking Refuge in the Three Jewels, we will not be able to have a high level of realization of bodhichitta. It is for this reason that the distinction between a practicing Buddhist and a non-Buddhist is made on the basis of whether or not an individual has taken Refuge in the Three Jewels.

However, when we talk about Taking Refuge in the Three Jewels, we should not imagine that it simply involves a ceremony in which we formally take Refuge from a master. There is a formal Refuge ceremony in Buddhism, but the ceremony is not the point. The point is that as a result of your own reflection, even without a master, you become fully convinced of the validity of the Buddha, Dharma and Sangha as the true ultimate objects of refuge, and that is when you actually become a Buddhist. You entrust your spiritual wellbeing to the Three Jewels, and this is what is really meant by Taking Refuge. On the other hand, if there is any doubt or apprehension in your mind about the validity of Buddha, Dharma and Sangha as being the ultimate objects of refuge, even though you may have taken part in a Refuge ceremony, that very doubt prevents you from being a practising Buddhist, at least for the time being. It is therefore important to understand what these objects of refuge are.

When we speak about Buddha in this context, we should not confine our understanding of the word to the historical person who came to India. Rather, our understanding of buddhahood[2] should be based on levels of spiritual realization. We should understand that buddhahood is a spiritual state of being. This is why the Buddhist scriptures can speak about past buddhas, buddhas of the present and buddhas of the future.

Now the next question is: how does a buddha come into being? How does a person become fully enlightened? When we reflect on buddhahood, we are bound to ask ourselves whether or not it is possible for an individual to attain such a state, to become a fully enlightened being, a buddha. Here we find that the key lies in understanding the nature of Dharma. If the Dharma exists, then the Sangha will certainly exist – the Sangha are those who have engaged in the path of the Dharma, and who have realized and actualized its truth. If there are Sangha members who have reached spiritual states where they have overcome at least the gross levels of negativity and afflictive emotions, then we can envision the possibility of attaining a freedom from negativity and afflictive emotions which is total. That state is what we call buddhahood.

In the present context, I think we must make a distinction between the use of "Dharma" as a generic term and its use in the specific framework of the Refuge. Generically, it refers to the scriptural Dharma – the Buddha's teaching and the spiritual realizations based on the practice of that teaching. In relation to the Refuge it has two aspects: one is the path that leads to the cessation of suffering and afflictive emotions, and the other is cessation[3] itself. It is only by understanding true cessation and the path leading to cessation that we can have some idea of what the state of liberation is.

DEPENDENT ORIGINATION

In the Sutras, Buddha stated several times that whoever perceives the interdependent nature of reality sees the Dharma; and whoever sees the Dharma sees the Buddha.[4] We find there are three levels of meaning here.

Firstly, the understanding of the principle of interdependent origination that is common to all Buddhist schools explains it in terms of causal dependence. This principle means that all conditioned things and events in the universe come into being only as a result of the interaction of various causes and conditions. This is significant because it precludes two possibilities. One is that things can arise from nowhere, with no causes and conditions, and the second is that things can arise on account of a transcendent creator. Both these possibilities are negated.

Secondly, we can understand the principle of dependent origination in terms of parts and whole. All material objects can be understood in terms of how the parts compose the whole, and how the very idea of "whole" depends upon the existence of parts. Such dependence clearly exists in the physical world. Similarly, non-physical entities, like consciousness, can be considered in terms of their temporal sequences: the idea of their wholeness is based upon the successive sequences that compose a continuum. So when we consider the universe in these terms, not only do we see each conditioned thing as dependently originated, we also understand that the entire phenomenal world arises according to the principle of dependent origination.

There is a third dimension to the meaning of dependent origination, which is that all things and events – everything, in fact – arise solely as a result of the mere coming together of the many factors which make them up. When you analyze things by mentally breaking them down into their constitutive parts, you come to the understanding that it is simply in dependence upon other factors that anything comes into being. Therefore there is nothing that has any independent or intrinsic identity of its own. Whatever identity we give things is contingent on the interaction between our perception and reality itself. However, this is not to say that things do not exist. Buddhism is not nihilistic. Things do exist, but they do not have an independent, autonomous reality.

Let us now refer back to the statement by the Buddha, when he said that seeing dependent origination leads to seeing the Dharma. There are three different meanings to this concept of Dharma which correspond to the three different levels of meaning of dependent origination.

Firstly, we can relate Dharma to the first level of meaning of dependent origination, which is causal dependence. By developing a deep understanding of the interdependent nature of reality in terms of causal dependence, we are able to appreciate the workings of what we call "karma", that is, the karmic law of cause and effect which governs human actions. This law explains how experiences of suffering arise as a result of negative actions, thoughts and behavior, and how desirable experiences such as joy arise as a result of the causes and conditions which correspond to that result – positive actions, emotions and thoughts.

Developing a deep understanding of dependent origination in terms of causal dependence gives you a fundamental insight into the nature of reality. When you realize that everything we experience arises as a result of the interaction and coming together of causes and conditions, your whole view changes. Your perspective on your own inner experiences, and the world at large, shifts as you begin to see everything in terms of this causal principle. Once you have developed that kind of outlook, you will be able to situate your understanding of karma within that framework, since karmic laws are a particular instance of this overall general causal principle.

Similarly, when you have a deep understanding of the other two dimensions of dependent origination – the dependence of parts and whole, and the interdependence between perception and existence – your view will deepen, and you will appreciate that there is a disparity between the way things appear to you and the way they actually are. What appears as some kind of autonomous, objective reality out there does not really fit with the actual nature of reality.

Once we appreciate that fundamental disparity between appearance and reality, we gain insight into the way our emotions work, and how we react to events and objects. Underlying the strong emotional responses we have to situations, we see that there is an assumption that some kind of independently existing reality exists out there. In this way, we develop an insight into the various functions of the mind and the different levels of consciousness within us. We also grow to understand that although certain types of mental states seem so real, and although objects appear to be so vivid, in reality they are mere illusions. They do not really exist in the way we think they do.

It is through this type of reflection and analysis that we will be able to gain an insight into what in technical Buddhist language is called "the origin of suffering", in other words, those emotional experiences that lead to confusion, and which afflict the mind. When this is combined with an understanding of the interdependent nature of reality at the subtlest level, then we also gain insight into what we call "the empty nature of reality", by which we mean the way every object and event arises only as a combination of many factors, and has no independent or autonomous existence.

Our insight into emptiness will, of course, help us to understand that any ideas that are based on the contrary view, that things exist intrinsically and independently, are misapprehensions.

They are misunderstandings of the nature of reality. We realize that they have no valid grounding either in reality or in our own valid experience, whereas the empty nature of reality has a valid grounding both in logical reasoning and in our experience. Gradually, we come to appreciate that it is possible to arrive at a state of knowledge where such misapprehension is eliminated completely; that is cessation.

In *Clear Words,* Chandrakirti states that if one can posit emptiness, then one can posit the world of dependent origination. If one can posit that, then one can posit the causal relationship between suffering and its origin. Once one accepts this, then one can also conceive of and accept the possibility that there could be an end to suffering. If one can do that, argues Chandrakirti, then one can also accept that it is possible for individuals to realize and actualize that state. Finally, of course, one can conceive of buddhas who have actually perfected that state of cessation.

The point is that by developing a profound understanding of the principle of dependent origination, we can understand both the truth of the subtle origins of suffering, and the truth of cessation. This is the meaning of Buddha's statement, that by understanding dependent origination, we see the Dharma. In this way we can see the truth of cessation and the path that leads to that cessation. Once we understand these, we are able to conceive that it is possible for Sangha members to realize and actualize these states, and for buddhas to perfect them. Finally, we come to some understanding of what buddhahood really means.

THE TWO TRUTHS

In order to develop a comprehensive understanding of the Four Noble Truths, it is also necessary to be familiar with the Two Truths, conventional or relative truth, and ultimate truth.

So how can we develop a personal understanding of the fundamental Buddhist doctrine of the Two Truths? By coming to know our everyday world of lived experience, we appreciate what is known as samvaharasatya, the world of conventional reality, where the causal principle operates. If we accept the reality of this world as conventional, then we can accept the empty nature of this world which, according to Buddhism, is the ultimate truth, the paramarthasatya. The relationship between these two aspects of reality is important. The world of appearance is used not so much as a contrast or an opposite to the world of ultimate truth, but rather as the evidence, the very basis on which the ultimate nature of reality is established.

Only when you have an understanding of the nature and relationship of these Two Truths are you in a position to fully understand the meaning of the Four Noble Truths. And once you understand the Four Noble Truths, then you have a sound foundation on which to develop a good understanding of what is meant by Taking Refuge in the Three Jewels.

THE FOUR NOBLE TRUTHS

THE FOUR NOBLE TRUTHS
PROVIDE AN UNDERSTANDING
OF THE RELATIONSHIP BETWEEN
CAUSES AND THEIR EFFECTS

Previous photograph, a prostrating pilgrim in front of the Potala Palace, Lhasa, Tibet.

Left, Pilgrim in traditional costume, holding a mala (prayer beads) at Reting Monastery, Tibet.

Now let us turn to the Buddhist teaching on the Four Noble Truths. The first question we might ask is why these Truths are considered to be so fundamental, and why, in fact, Buddha taught them at all.

In order to answer this, we have to relate the Four Noble Truths to our own experience as individual human beings. It is a fact – a natural fact of life – that each one of us has an innate desire to seek happiness and to overcome suffering. This is something very instinctive, and there is no need to prove it is there. Happiness is something that we all aspire to achieve, and of course we naturally have a right to fulfil that aspiration. In the same way, suffering is something everybody wishes to avoid, and we also have the right to try to overcome suffering. So if this aspiration to achieve happiness and overcome suffering is our natural state of being, and our natural quest, the question is how we should go about fulfilling that aspiration.

This leads us to the teachings on the Four Noble Truths, which provide an understanding of the relationship between two sets of events: causes and their effects. On one side we have suffering, but suffering does not come from nowhere, it arises as a result of its own causes and conditions. On the other side we have happiness, which also arises from its own particular set of causes and conditions.

Now when we speak of happiness in Buddhism, our understanding of it is not confined to a state of feeling. Certainly

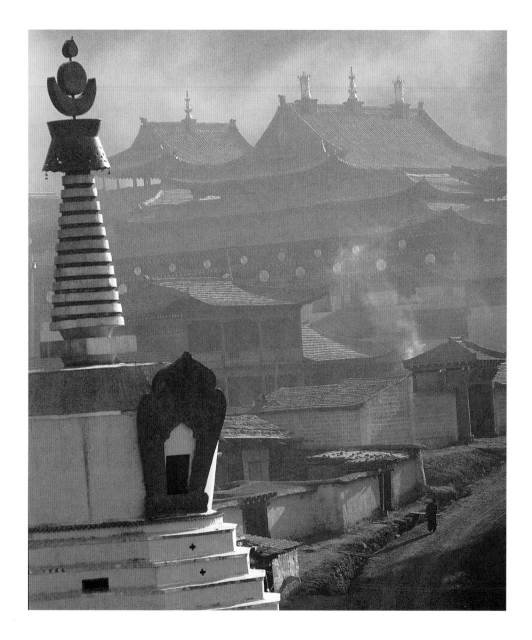

cessation (the total cessation of suffering) is not a state of feeling, and yet we could say that cessation is the highest form of happiness because it is, by definition, complete freedom from suffering. Here again cessation, or true happiness, does not come into being from nowhere or without any cause. This is a subtle point, of course, because from the Buddhist perspective cessation is not a conditioned event, so it cannot be said to be actually produced, or caused, by anything. However, the actualization or attainment of cessation does depend on the path and on an individual's effort. You cannot attain cessation without making an effort. In this sense we can therefore say that the path that leads to cessation is the cause of cessation.

Above, monks going to perform puja (an offering ceremony) at Labrang Monastery.

Left, Chorten (reliquary) beside Langmusi Monastery, Eastern Tibet.

The teachings on the Four Noble Truths clearly distinguish two sets of causes and effects: those causes which produce suffering, and those which produce happiness. By showing us how to distinguish these in our own lives, the teachings aim at nothing less than to enable us to fulfill our deepest aspiration – to be happy and to overcome suffering.

Once we have realized that this is why Buddha taught the Four Noble Truths, we might go on to ask ourselves the reason for their specific sequence: why are the Four Noble Truths taught in a particular order, starting with suffering, continuing with the origin of suffering, and so on? On this point we should understand that the order in which the Four Noble Truths are taught has nothing to do with the order in which things arise in reality. Rather, it is related to the way an individual should go about practicing the Buddhist path, and attain realizations based on that practice.

In the *Uttaratantra*, Maitreya states that there are four stages to curing an illness.

66 **Just as the disease needs be diagnosed, its cause eliminated, a healthy state achieved and the remedy implemented, so also should suffering, its causes, its cessation and the path be known, removed, attained and undertaken.**[1] 99

Maitreya uses the analogy of a sick person to explain the way in which realizations based on the Four Noble Truths can be attained. In order for a sick person to get well, the first

Left, Mandala
in the roof of
a chorten in
Purne Village,
Zanskar, India.

step is that he or she must know that he is ill, otherwise the desire to be cured will not arise. Once you have acknowledged that you are sick, then naturally you will try to find out what led to it and what makes your condition even worse. When you have identified these, you will gain an understanding of whether or not the illness can be cured, and a wish to be free from the illness will arise in you. In fact this is not just a mere wish, because once you have recognized the conditions that led to your illness, your desire to be free of it will be much stronger since that knowledge will give you a confidence and conviction that you can overcome the illness. With that conviction, you will want to take all the medications and remedies necessary.

In the same way, unless you know that you are suffering, your desire to be free from suffering will not arise in the first place. So the first step we must take as practising Buddhists is to recognize our present state as *duhkha* or suffering, frustration and unsatisfactoriness. Only then will we wish to look into the causes and conditions that give rise to suffering.

It is very important to understand the context of the Buddhist emphasis on recognizing that we are all in a state of suffering, otherwise there is a danger we could misunderstand the Buddhist outlook, and think that it involves rather morbid thinking, a basic pessimism and almost an obsessiveness about the reality of suffering. The reason why Buddha laid so much emphasis on developing insight into the nature

of suffering is because there is an alternative – there is a way out, it is actually possible to free oneself from it. This is why it is so crucial to realize the nature of suffering, because the stronger and deeper your insight into suffering is, the stronger your aspiration to gain freedom from it becomes. So the Buddhist emphasis on the nature of suffering should be seen within this wider perspective, where there is an appreciation of the possibility of complete freedom from suffering. If we had no concept of liberation, then to spend so much time reflecting on suffering would be utterly pointless.

We could say that the two sets of causes and effects I mentioned earlier refer, on the one hand, to the process of an

" **This is why it is so crucial to realize the nature of suffering, because the stronger and deeper your insight into suffering is, the stronger your aspiration to gain freedom from it becomes.** "

unenlightened existence, which relates to the causal chain between suffering and its origins, and, on the other hand, to the process of an enlightened existence which pertains to the causal links between the path and true cessation. When the

Left, Monk beside large prayer wheel in Sakya Monastery, Tibet.

Buddha elaborated on these two processes, he taught what is called the doctrine of the Twelve Links of Dependent Origination, or Twelve Nidanas[2].

The nidanas are the Twelve Links in the cycle of existence, which goes from ignorance, to volition, to consciousness, and so on, all the way to old age and death. When the causal process of an unenlightened existence is described in detail – that is, a life which is led within the framework of suffering and its origin – then the sequence of the Twelve Links begins with ignorance, and proceeds with volition, consciousness and so on. This sequence describes how an individual sentient being, as a result of certain causes and conditions, enters into the process of unenlightened existence.

However, if that same individual engages in certain spiritual practices, he or she can reverse this process, and the alternative sequence is that of the process which leads to enlightenment. For example, if the continuum of ignorance comes to an end then the continuum of volitional actions will cease. If that ceases, then the consciousness that serves as the support for such actions will cease; and so on.

You can see that the teachings on the Twelve Links of Dependent Origination are in some sense an elaboration on the two sets of causes and conditions described by the Four Noble Truths.

THE TRUTH OF SUFFERING

THE FIRST OF THE
FOUR NOBLE TRUTHS

Previous photograph,
Monks playing dung-
chen at Nechung
Monastery, Tibet.

Above, women
weeding the barley
fields near Phuktal
Monastery, Zanskar,
India.

Left, Monk walking by
a prayer hall, Ganden
Monastery, Tibet.

The first of the Four Noble Truths is the Truth of Suffering.

The various philosophical schools of Buddhism interpret the word 'truth' in different ways. For example, there is a fundamental difference between the Prasangika Madhyamaka school and the Shravakayana schools in the way they distinguish ordinary beings from Arya or superior beings. The Shravakayana makes the distinction on the basis of whether or not a person has gained direct intuitive insight into the Four Noble Truths. The Prasangika Madhyamikas do not accept this criterion, because they hold that even ordinary beings can have direct intuitive realizations of the Four Noble Truths. However, I will not go into these arguments here because it would complicate my explanation.

Instead, we will turn straightaway to the meaning of *duhkha* or suffering. In this context, duhkha is the ground or basis of painful experience, and refers generally to our state of existence as conditioned by karma, delusions and afflictive emotions. As Asanga states in the *Compendium of Knowledge (Abhidharmasamuchchaya)*, the concept of duhkha must embrace both the environment where we live and the individual beings living within it.

THE THREE REALMS OF SUFFERING

In order to understand the environment in which unenlightened beings live, we must look briefly at Buddhist cosmology.[1] According to the Buddhist teachings, there are Three Realms of existence: the Desire Realm, the Form Realm, and the Formless Realm[2].

The difficulty here, for most of us, is how to understand these Three Realms. In particular, how should we conceive of form realms and formless realms? It is not enough to simply say that Buddha talked about these in the scriptures – that alone is not a sufficient reason for a Buddhist to accept their existence. Perhaps the most helpful approach is to understand these realms in terms of different levels of consciousness. For example, according to Buddhism, the very distinction between enlightened existence and unenlightened existence is made on the basis of the respective levels of consciousness. A person whose mind is undisciplined and untamed is in the state of samsara or suffering; whereas someone whose mind is disciplined and tamed is in the state of nirvana, or ultimate peace.

We also find that the Buddhist distinction between ordinary and Arya beings is made on the basis of their respective levels of consciousness or realization. Anyone who has gained direct intuitive realization of emptiness, or the ultimate nature of reality, is said to be an Arya according to

Right, Barley fields near Phuktal Monastery, Zanskar, India.

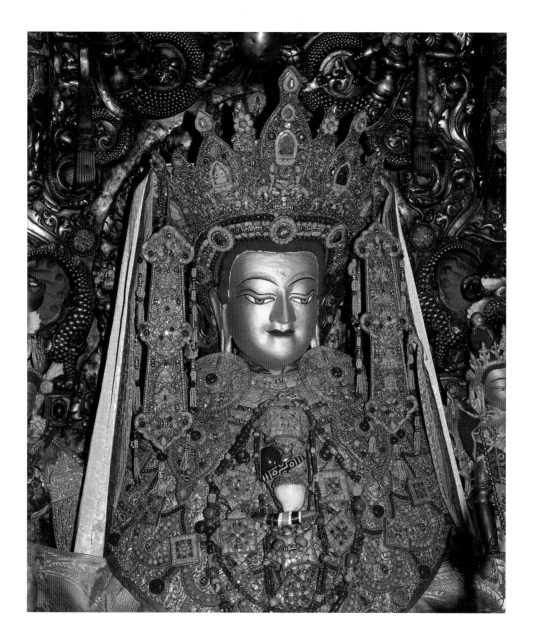

Mahayana, and anyone who has not gained that realization is called an ordinary being. In relation to the Three Realms, the subtler the level of consciousness an individual attains, the subtler the realm of existence he can inhabit.

For example, if a person's ordinary mode of being is very much within the context of desire and attachment then such attachment to physical objects, thought processes and sensory experiences leads to a form of existence which is confined within the Desire Realm, both now and in the future. At the same time, there are people who have transcended attachment to objects of immediate perception and to physical sensations, but who are attached to the inner states of joy or bliss. That type of person creates causes that will lead him or her to future rebirths where physical existence has a much more refined form.

Furthermore, there are those who have transcended attachment not only to physical sensations but to pleasurable inner sensations of joy and bliss, too. They tend more towards a state of equanimity. Their level of consciousness is much subtler than the other two, but they are still attached to a particular mode of being. The grosser levels of their mind can lead to the Fourth Level of the Form Realm, while the subtler attachment towards equanimity leads to the Formless Realms. So this is the way we relate the Three Realms to levels of consciousness.

Left, Statue of Jowo Sakyamuni, Jokhang Temple, Lhasa.

On the basis of this cosmology, Buddhism talks about the infinite process of the universe, coming into being and going through a process of dissolution before again coming into being. This process has to be understood in relation to the Three Realms of existence. According to the Sarvastivadin

> 66 **Buddhism talks about the infinite process of the universe, coming into being and going through a process of dissolution before again coming into being.** 99

Abhidharma literature[3] (the Buddhist discourses on meta-physics and psychology which serve as a reference in Tibetan Buddhism), it is from the Third Level of the Form Realm downwards that the world is subject to the continuous process of arising and dissolution. From the Fourth Level of the Form Realm upwards, which includes the Formless Realm, the world is beyond this process which we could call the evolution of the physical universe.

This infinite process of evolution is very similar to the modern scientific notion of the Big Bang. If the scientific cosmological theory of the Big Bang accepts only one Big Bang as *the* beginning of everything, then of course that

would not fit with basic Buddhist cosmology. In this case, Buddhists would have to bite their nails and come up with some way of explaining how the Big Bang does not contradict the Buddhist idea of the evolutionary process of the universe. However, if the Big Bang theory does not entail only one Big Bang at the beginning, but accepts a multiplicity of Big Bangs, then that would correspond very well to the Buddhist understanding of the evolutionary process.

The Sarvastivadin Abhidharma also discusses the precise ways in which the universe dissolves at the end of each cycle. When the physical universe is destroyed by fire it is destroyed only below the first level of the Form Realm; when it is destroyed by water it dissolves from the second level of the Form Realm downwards; when it is destroyed by wind, it is destroyed from the third level of the Form Realm downwards. In Buddhist cosmology, therefore, the evolution of the physical universe is understood in terms of the four elements of fire, water, wind and earth. In general, we usually add space to this list, making a total of five elements. A complex discussion on the elemental mechanics of dissolution can be found not only in the Abhidharma but also in the *Uttaratantra*. These explanations seem to be very similar to modern scientific theories.

Having said this, what is stated in the Abhidharma literature does not always have to be taken literally. According to the Abhidharma, for example, the structure of the universe is

Left, Doorway to building in Dhankar monastery, Spiti, Himachal Pradesh, India.

Above, Khampa
woman with
colorful jewellery
beneath the Potala
Palace, Lhasa, Tibet.

Left, Monk
looking over
the Lhasa valley
from Drepung
Monastery, Tibet.

based on the model of a Mount Meru in the centre, surrounded by four "continents". We also find that many of the Abhidharmic descriptions of the size of the sun and moon contradict modern scientific explanations. Given that scientific experiments have proved these claims to be wrong, we will have to accept the conclusion of the scientists on these points.

So here I have outlined very briefly how Buddhism understands the evolution of the physical universe, or, in a broad sense, the environment. As for the sentient beings that inhabit these environments, Buddhism accepts many different types. There are beings with bodily forms and beings which are perceived as formless. Even in the world with which we are familiar, there are many beings which are perceptible to our senses and some which are not, like those of the spirit world for example.

Generally speaking, the Buddhist understanding is that birth as a human being is one of the most ideal forms of existence because it is conducive to practising Dharma. So compared to human beings, spirits would in fact be considered inferior because that form of existence is less effective for pursuing the practice of Dharma. Spirits may have certain abilities that are not open to us, like certain powers of precognition or some supernatural powers, but the fact remains that they are part of this world where human beings also live. All beings in this world are under the control of delusion and afflictive emotions. In some sense one could say that they are

actually the products of delusion and afflictive emotions.

Lama Tsongkhapa describes very vividly the unenlightened existence of sentient beings in samsara. He uses the analogy of someone being tied up very tightly by the ropes of negative karma, delusions, afflictive emotions and thoughts. Encased in this tight net of ego and self-grasping, they are tossed around aimlessly by the currents of fluctuating experiences, of suffering and pain[4]. This is what samsaric life is like.

Left, Mandala in the roof of chorten at the site of the former western gate of Lhasa, Tibet.

THREE TYPES OF SUFFERING

So now the question is, what is duhkha? What is suffering? Buddhism describes three levels or types of suffering. The first is called "the suffering of suffering", the second, "the suffering of change", and the third is "the suffering of conditioning".

When we talk about the first type, the suffering of suffering, we are talking in very conventional terms of experiences which we would all identify as suffering. These experiences are painful. In Buddhism there are four main experiences of this type of suffering which are considered to be fundamental to life in samsara: the sufferings of birth, sickness, ageing and death. The significance of recognizing these states as forms of suffering, and the importance of this recognition as a catalyst of the spiritual quest, is very strongly demonstrated in the Buddha's own life story. According to the story, when he was the young Prince Siddhartha, the Buddha is said to have caught sight of a sick person, an old person, and a dead person being carried away. The impact of seeing this suffering apparently led him to the realization that so long as he was not free of the infinite process of birth, he would always be subject to these other three sufferings. Later, the sight of a spiritual aspirant is supposed to have made the Buddha fully aware that there is a possibility of freedom from this cycle of suffering.

❝ The sight of a spiritual aspirant is supposed to have made the Buddha fully aware that there is a possibility of freedom from the cycle of suffering. ❞

Right, Monk prostrating in the courtyard of the Jokhang Temple, Lhasa, Tibet.

So in Buddhism there is an understanding that so long as we are subject to the process of rebirth, all other forms of suffering are natural consequences of that initial starting point. We could characterize our life as being within the cycle of birth and death, and sandwiched in between these two, as it were, are the various sufferings related to illness and ageing.

The second level of suffering, the suffering of change, refers to experiences we ordinarily identify as pleasurable.

However, in reality, as long as we are in an unenlightened state, all our joyful experiences are tainted and ultimately bring suffering.

Why does Buddhism claim that experiences which are apparently pleasurable are ultimately states of suffering? The point is that we perceive them as states of pleasure or joy only because, in comparison to painful experiences,

they appear as a form of relief. Their pleasurable status is only relative. If they were truly joyful states in themselves, then just as painful experiences increase the more we indulge in the causes that lead to pain, likewise, the more we engage in the causes that give rise to pleasurable experience, our pleasure or joy should intensify; but this is not the case.

On an everyday level, for example, when you have good food, nice clothes, attractive jewellery and so on, for a short time you feel really marvellous. Not only do you enjoy a feeling of satisfaction, but when you show your things to others, they share in it too. But then one day passes, one week passes, one month passes, and the very same object that once gave you such pleasure might simply cause you frustration. That is the nature of things – they change. The same also applies to fame. At the beginning you might think to yourself, "Oh! I'm so happy! Now I have a good name, I'm famous!" But after some time, it could be that all you feel is frustration and dissatisfaction. The same sort of change can

Above, Close-up of a monk in Sera Monastery, Tibet.

Left, Monks on the roof of the Jokhang Temple, Lhasa, Tibet.

happen in friendships and in sexual relationships. At the beginning you almost go mad with passion, but later that very passion can turn to hatred and aggression, and, in the worst cases, even lead to murder. So that is the nature of things. If you look carefully, everything beautiful and good, everything that we consider desirable, brings us suffering in the end.

Finally, we come to the third type of suffering, the suffering of conditioning. This addresses the main question: why is this the nature of things? The answer is, because everything that happens in samsara is due to ignorance. Under the influence or control of ignorance, there is no possibility of a permanent state of happiness. Some kind of trouble, some kind of problem, always arises. So long as we remain under the power of ignorance, that is, our fundamental misapprehension or confusion about the nature of things, then sufferings come one after another, like ripples on water.

The third level of suffering, therefore, refers to the bare fact of our unenlightened existence, which is under the influence of this fundamental confusion and of the negative karmas to which confusion gives rise. The reason it is called the suffering of conditioning is because this state of existence serves as the basis not only for painful experiences in this life, but also for the causes and conditions of suffering in the future.

Dharmakirti's *Commentary on the Compendium of Valid Cognition (Pramanavarttika)* and Aryadeva's *Four Hundred*

Right, Barley fields and village at dusk near Phuktal Monastery Zanskar, India.

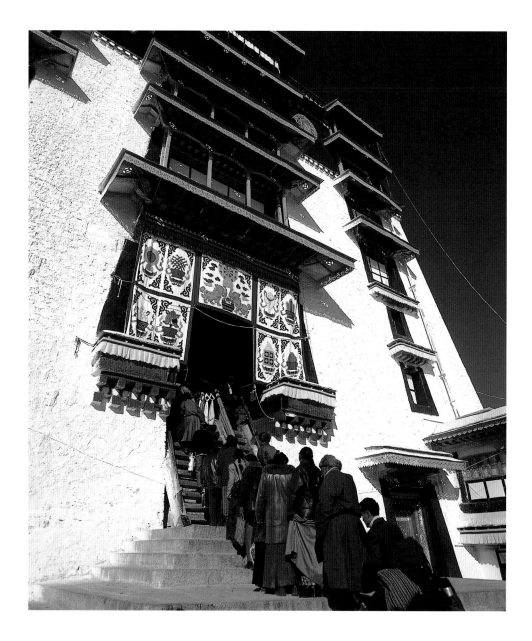

Verses on the Middle Way (Chatuhshatakashastrakarika) both offer a useful way of looking at this third level of suffering, and help deepen our understanding of it. Both works lay the emphasis on reflecting upon the subtle level of the transient, impermanent nature of reality.

It is important to bear in mind that there are two levels of meaning here. One can understand impermanence in terms of how something arises, stays for a while, and then disappears. This level of impermanence can be understood quite easily. We should add that on this level, the dissolution of something requires a secondary condition which acts as a catalyst to destroy its continuity. However, there is also a second, more subtle understanding of transience. From this more subtle perspective, the obvious process of change we have just described is merely the effect of a deeper, underlying and dynamic process of change. At a deeper level, everything is changing from moment to moment, constantly. This process of momentary change is not due to a secondary condition that arises to destroy something, but rather the very cause that led a thing to arise is also the cause of its destruction. In other words, within the cause of its origin lies the cause of its cessation.

Momentariness should thus be understood in two ways. First, in terms of the three moments of existence of any entity – in the first instant, it arises; in the second instant, it stays; in the third instant, it dissolves. Second, in terms of each

Left, Pilgrims waiting to enter the Potala Palace on Tibetan New Year's Day 2000. New Year's Day is the one day of the year the public can enter the Potala free of charge.

59

Left, Woman adjusting the jewellery of her friend whilst waiting for the arrival of the Dalai Lama at Kungri village in Spiti, Himachal Pradesh, India.

instant itself. An instant is not static; as soon as it arises, it moves towards its own cessation.

Since everything arises complete from the outset, the birth of things comes together with the seed or potential for their dissolution. In this respect, one could say that their cessation does not depend on any secondary, further condition. Therefore, in Buddhism, all phenomena are said to be "other-powered", that is, they are under the control of their causes.

Once you have developed this understanding of the transient nature of phenomena, you are able to situate the understanding you have of duhkha within that context, and reflect upon your life as an individual in this samsaric world. You know that since the world has come into being as a result of its own causes and conditions, it too must be other-powered. In other words, it must be under the control of the causal processes that led to its arising. However, in the context of samsara, the causes that we are referring to here are nothing other than our fundamental confusion or ignorance (*marigpa* in Tibetan), and the delusory states to which confusion gives rise. We know that so long as we are under the domination of this fundamental confusion, there is no room for lasting joy or happiness. Of course, within the Three Realms there are states which are comparatively more joyful than others. However, so long as we remain within samsara, whether in the Form Realm, the Formless Realm or the Desire Realm, there is no scope for joy to be lasting. In the final

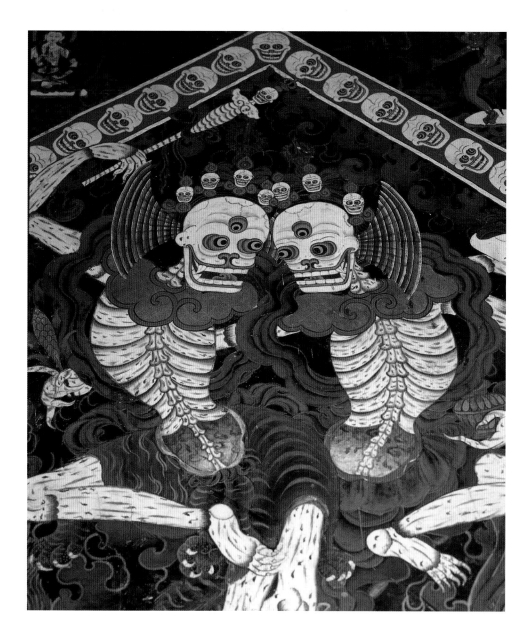

analysis, we are in a state of duhkha. This is the meaning of the third type of suffering.

IGNORANCE

The Sanskrit word for ignorance or confusion is avidya, which literally means "not knowing". There are several interpretations of what is meant by avidya according to the different philosophical schools and their various views of the fundamental Buddhist doctrine of anatman or no-self. However, the general meaning that is common to all the schools is an understanding that there lies a fundamental ignorance at the root of our existence. The reason for this is quite simple. We all know from personal experience that what we deeply aspire to gain is happiness and what we try to avoid is suffering. Yet our actions and our behaviour only lead to more suffering and not to the lasting joy and happiness that we seek. This must surely mean that we are operating within the framework of ignorance. This is how we experience the fundamental confusion at the root of our life.

One way to reflect on the nature of duhkha, according to the traditional Buddhist teachings, is to reflect on the sufferings endured in each of the six "realms" of the samsaric world system.[5] These include the hell realms, the animal realm, the realm of pretas or hungry ghosts, and so on. For some people, such

Left, painting of dancing skeletons, the guardians of the cemetaries, on the walls of Meru Nyingba Monastery, Lhasa, Tibet.

Left, Lamayuru
Monastery in
the hills of the
Indus Valley,
Ladakh, India.

reflections may spur them to deepen their quest for freedom from suffering. However, for many other people, including myself, it can be more effective to reflect on our own human suffering. Although Buddhism teaches that human life is one of the most positive of all forms of life, since human beings have the potential to gain perfect enlightenment, it is not always that joyful. We are subject to the unavoidable sufferings of birth, death, aging and sickness. In addition, when one reflects on the fact that life is conditioned and dominated by confusion, and the delusory emotions and thoughts to which confusion gives rise, then for someone like myself it seems much more effective to recognize this than to think about the sufferings of other realms.

As I mentioned before, the Buddhist scriptures describe the causal process through which ignorance gives rise to volitional acts, which in turn give rise to a birth in one of the samsaric worlds, and so on, as the Twelve Links in the Chain of Dependent Origination. On this, Buddha made three observations. He said that:

❝ Because there is this, that ensues. Because this came into being, that came into being. Because there is fundamental ignorance, volitional acts come into being.[6] ❞

When commenting upon these three statements, Asanga explains in the *Compendium of Knowledge* that Three Conditions are necessary for anything to arise, and I think an understanding of these would be useful here.

Because there is this, that ensues

Asanga explained that the significance of the first statement is that all phenomena come into being because they have causes. One could say there is an infinite causal chain. It is not as if there were a first cause, or a "beginning" point in time, from which everything arose. Asanga referred to that observation as the **Condition of the Existence of a Cause.**

Because this came into being, that came into being

When commenting on the second statement, Asanga introduced what he called the **Condition of Impermanence.** The meaning of this is that the mere fact that something exists is not sufficient for it to produce an effect. For something to have the potential to produce an effect, it must itself be subject to causation; in other words, it must come into being itself as a result of other causes. Hence we have an infinity of causes. So mere existence alone does not give rise to consequences; a cause should not only exist, it should also be impermanent and subject to causation.

Right, Young man throwing paper prayer flags ("windhorses") beside new prayer flags on Bompori Hill above Lhasa, Tibet as part of the Tibetan New Year festival.

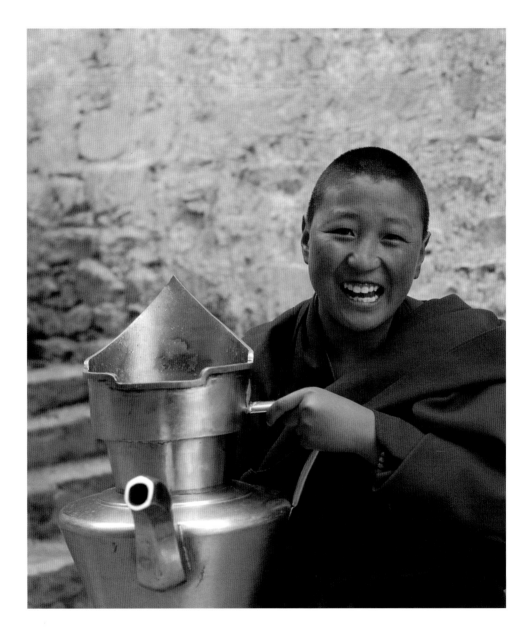

Because there is fundamental ignorance, volitional acts come into being

Asanga's comment on this mentions a further qualification that is needed for a cause to produce an effect, which he calls the **Condition of Potentiality**. The idea is that it is not sufficient for a cause to exist and to be impermanent for it to produce a particular result. It is not the case that everything can produce everything or anything. There must be some kind of natural correlation between a cause and its effect. For example, because the nature of our life is suffering we desire happiness, yet out of ignorance we create more suffering for ourselves, and this is because suffering is the root of our life. The result we obtain thus correlates with its cause.

Furthermore, there are different ways in which conditions can effect a result. These have more to do with the complex functioning of the mind. The scriptures identify five types of condition, such as the objective condition, which refers to the object of perception; the sensory organs that give rise to sensory perception; the immediately preceding condition, which is the earlier continuum of your consciousness; and so on. So you can see that the Buddhist understanding of causation is highly complex.

Let us take the example of fire. What would the material cause of fire be? We could say that a potential exists within the fuel that is used to make a fire, which then becomes the fire.

Left, Young monk with a large pot of butter tea for refilling other monks' cups during morning prayers at Ganden Monastery, Tibet.

Left, Mother with child spinning large prayer wheels while doing circumambulation of Langmusi Monastery, Eastern Tibet.

In the case of consciousness, the issue is more complex. For example, it is obvious that we need the physical sensory organs for sensory perceptions to take place. Of course, the physical basis of consciousness would also include the nervous system, although in the classic Buddhist scriptures there is hardly any discussion of this, and it is perhaps something that needs to be added to Buddhist theories of epistemology and psychology. However, the substantial cause of consciousness would not be these physical entities. It has to be understood in terms of its own continuum, be it in the form of a potential or propensity or whatever. This is a very difficult topic, but perhaps we can say that the substantial cause of consciousness can be understood as the continuum of the subtle consciousness, although we should be careful not to end up in a position which implies that the material cause of anything is exactly the same as the thing itself. This would be untenable. We cannot maintain the position, for instance, that the substantial causes of sensory perceptions are always sensory perceptions, because sensory consciousnesses are gross levels of consciousness and are contingent on the physical organs of the individual, whereas the continuum should be understood on the level of the subtle consciousness. So perhaps we could say that the substantial causes of consciousness are present in the form of a potential rather than as actual conscious states.

CONSCIOUSNESS

When we talk about consciousness, or *shes pa* in Tibetan, we are not talking about a single, unitary, monolithic entity that is "out there". We are referring, of course, to the mental consciousness which is the sixth consciousness according to Buddhist psychology.[7]

Generally speaking, when we try to investigate our mind through introspection, we find that it tends to be dominated either by discursive thoughts or by feelings and sensations. So let us try to examine how feelings and discursive thoughts occur within the mind.

Right, Smoke hangs over monks in the courtyard of Nechung Monastery, Tibet before a ceremony as part of the Tibetan New Year Festival.

❝ When we try to investigate our mind through introspection, we find that it tends to be dominated either by discursive thoughts or by feelings and sensations. ❞

Feelings, of course, can be considered in relation to two different dimensions of reality. We can speak about them purely at the physical level, as sensations, but when we try to understand feelings in terms of mental consciousness the issue is far more complex. And although we naturally accept

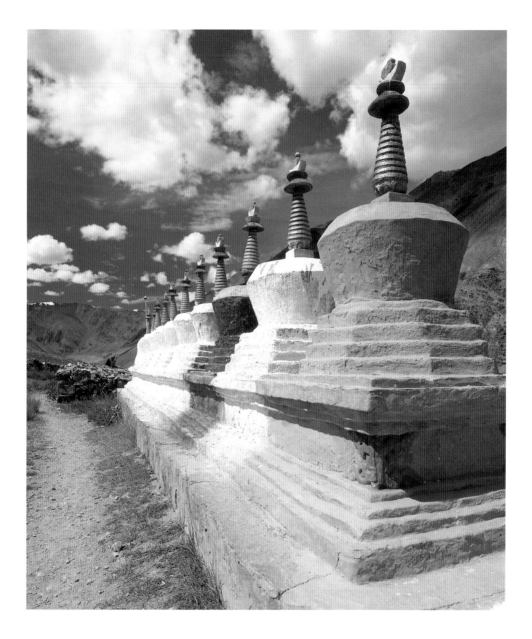

that there must be connections between the consciousness and the nervous system of the body, we must somehow be able to account for deeper levels of feeling as well, or what we could call tones of experience.

I would like to point out that although very little research has been carried out in this area, and despite the fact that what little exists is still at a rudimentary stage, experiments done on meditators point to a phenomenon which may be difficult to account for within the current scientific paradigm. These experiments have shown that without any voluntary physical change in the body, and without any physical movement on the part of the individual, a person can affect his or her physiological state simply by using the power of the mind through a focused, single-pointed state. The physiological changes that take place are difficult to explain according to current assumptions about human physiology.

There is no doubt that our consciousness and all our experiences are contingent upon our body, so the human mind and the human body are in some sense inextricable. Yet at the same time, I feel that research seems to point to the possibility that the human mind also has a power of its own which can be enhanced through reflection and meditation, or training of the mind. Furthermore, it is well known that there is a growing recognition

Left, Rows of chortens outside Testa village, Zanskar, India.

Below, Sangke grasslands near Labrang monastery, Eastern Tibet.

75

Left, Family
plowing barley
fields Lahtse, Tibet.

within modern medicine of the power of the will in the healing process. A person's willpower affects his physiology. How is willpower developed? It can be through thinking something through and discovering the reasonable grounds for one's understanding. It can also be through meditation. In whichever way it is developed, it is now acknowledged that the will can effect physical change.

What does this mean? What seems to be accepted scientifically is that all the thoughts that occur in our mind give rise to chemical changes and movements within the brain, which are then expressed in physiological change. But does pure thought lead to such physical effects too? And is it the case that thoughts occur solely as a result of chemical changes within the body or brain? I have asked scientists on several occasions whether it would be possible for the process to begin first with just pure thought, and then, secondly, thought processes occur which give rise to chemical changes, which in turn trigger physiological effects. Most of the time their answers have indicated that since it is assumed that consciousness is contingent upon a physical base (the brain, for instance), every occurrence of thought must necessarily be accompanied or caused by chemical changes in the brain. To me, however, that assumption seems to be based more on prejudice than experimental proof. I therefore think the question is still open and further research is needed, particularly involving practitioners who engage in profound meditation.

The Vajrayana literature contains discussions of the existence of different levels of consciousness, or different subtleties of mind, and the ways in which these correspond to subtle levels of energy. I think these explanations can contribute a great deal to our understanding of the nature of mind and its functions.

> " It is very difficult for us to glimpse the actual nature of conciousness, which is the sheer state of knowing or the luminosity of mind. "

So, as we saw earlier, most of our conscious mind consists either of states related with objects that we have experienced in the past – recollections of past experiences inform our present consciousness – or it consists of some kind of feeling or sensation. As a result, it is very difficult for us to glimpse the actual nature of consciousness, which is the sheer state of knowing or the luminosity of mind. One technique that we can use in order to do this is sitting meditation, through which we free our mind from thoughts of past experiences and from any form of anticipation of the future. Instead, we abide in the nowness of the present,

Right, Monk carrying prayer books. Phuktal Monastery, Zanskar, India.

Above, Nun in
Tidrum Nunnery,
Tibet.

Left, Devotee
spinning prayer
wheels while
performing
circumambulation
around Langmusi
Monastery,
Eastern Tibet.

although we cannot really talk of a "present" consciousness.

When you are able to clear away thoughts of the past and the future, slowly you begin to get a sense of the space between the two. You learn to abide in that present moment. In that space, you begin to glimpse what we call emptiness, and if you can remain in that emptiness for longer and longer periods of time then gradually the nature of consciousness itself, which is the sheer luminosity and natural awareness of mind, will slowly dawn in you. Through repeated practice this period can be lengthened more and more, so that your awareness of the nature of consciousness becomes clearer and clearer.

However, it is important to realize that this experience of the luminosity of mind, of the nature of mind, is not a profound realization in itself. Rebirth in many of the Formless Realms of samsara is considered to result from abiding in such states of clarity. On the other hand, if we know how to use that initial experience of luminosity as a basis, then we can build on it by complementing our meditation with other practices, and in this way it will become truly profound.

So here I have explained how we can look at the Buddha's teaching on the Truth of Suffering. Once you have developed this kind of recognition of the duhkha nature of life, you already have some understanding that at the root of our suffering lies a fundamental ignorance. This, of course, leads us to the Second Truth which is the Origin of Suffering.

THE TRUTH OF
THE ORIGIN
OF SUFFERING

THE SECOND OF THE
FOUR NOBLE TRUTHS

In the previous chapter we looked at the fact that we all desire happiness and wish to overcome suffering, and how, despite this natural aspiration, we tend to create the conditions for more suffering because we do not know the way to create the causes for happiness. We found that at the root of this situation lies a fundamental confusion or, in Buddhist terminology, a fundamental ignorance. This confusion applies not only to the way things are but also to the way causes and effects relate to each other. Therefore, in Buddhism we talk about two types of ignorance, or avidya: ignorance of the laws of causality, specifically of the laws of karma, and ignorance of the ultimate nature of reality. These relate respectively to the two levels of understanding of dependent origination that we outlined in Chapter One. The first level was an understanding in terms of causal dependence, which dispels our ignorance of the laws of causality. The more profound level was an understanding in terms of the ultimate nature of reality, which dispels our fundamental ignorance.

However, this does not mean that ignorance is the only cause of our unenlightened existence. This has, of course, many other derivative causes and conditions, which are technically called kleshas or "afflictive emotions and thoughts". This is a very complex class of emotions and thoughts, described in detail in the Abhidharma literature. For example, according to Abhidharma there are six root afflictive emotions or thoughts, out of which arise 20 secondary types of

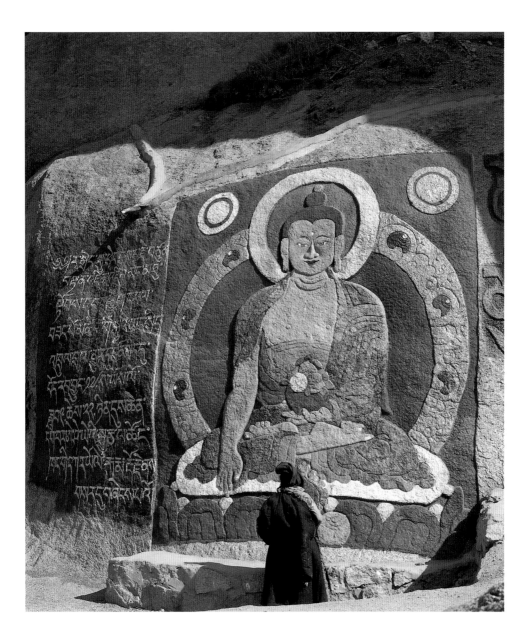

emotions and thoughts. The Abhidharma therefore presents a comprehensive explanation of the whole world of thought and emotion.

There is another explanation of the process of being in samsara in the Tantric Vajrayana literature, which details the 80 types of thoughts or concepts which are indicative of our being in an unenlightened state. The Kalachakra literature, which belongs to the Vajrayana class, further identifies the causes of samsaric existence in terms of propensities or natural dispositions.

These afflictive emotions and thoughts, which arise from our fundamental delusion, give rise to volitional actions. So together, delusions and karmic actions are the origins of our suffering.

Generally speaking, afflictive emotions and thoughts are defined as those of which the mere occurrence creates immediate disturbance within our mind. They then afflict us from within.

KARMA: CATEGORIES OF KARMIC ACTION

If that is the general definition of klesha, what is the definition of karma?[1] We should remember to situate karma within the context of the wider Buddhist understanding of the natural laws of causality. Karma is one particular instance of the natural causal laws that operate throughout the universe

where, according to Buddhism, things and events come into being purely as a result of the combination of causes and conditions.

Karma, then, is an instance of the general law of causality. What makes karma unique is that it involves intentional action, and therefore an agent. The natural causal processes operating in the world cannot be termed karmic where there is no agent involved. In order for a causal process to be a karmic one, it must involve an individual whose intention would lead to a particular action. It is this specific type of causal mechanism which is known as karma.

" Karma is an instance of the general law of causality. " "

Left, Pilgrim family doing circumambulation around Langmusi Monastery, Eastern Tibet.

So within the general field of karmic action we can talk about three different types of action which produce corresponding effects. Actions which produce suffering and pain are generally considered negative or non-virtuous actions. Actions that lead to positive and desirable consequences, such as experiences of joy and happiness, are considered to be positive or virtuous actions. The third category includes actions which lead to experiences of equanimity, or neutral feelings and experiences; these are considered to be neutral actions, and are neither virtuous nor non-virtuous.

In terms of the actual nature of karmic actions themselves, there are two principal types: mental acts – actions that are not necessarily manifested through physical action – and physical acts, which include both bodily and verbal acts. Then, from the point of view of the medium of expression of an action, we distinguish actions of the mind, of speech, and of the body. Furthermore, in the scriptures we also find discussions about karmic actions which are completely virtuous, completely non-virtuous, and those which are a mixture of the two. I feel that for many of us who practise the Dharma, most of our actions may be a mixture of the two.

If we analyze a single karmic action, we can see that there are several stages within that event. There is a beginning, which is the stage of the motivation or intention; there is the actual execution of the act; and then there is the culmination or completion of the act. According to the scriptures, the intensity and force of a karmic action vary according to the way each of these stages is carried out.

Let us take the example of a negative action. If, at the stage of motivation, the person has a very strong negative emotion like anger, and then acts on an impulse and carries out the action, but immediately afterwards feels deep regret for the action he has committed, all three stages would not be completely fulfilled. Consequently, the action would be

Right, Young monk in the doorway of Samye Monastery, Tibet.

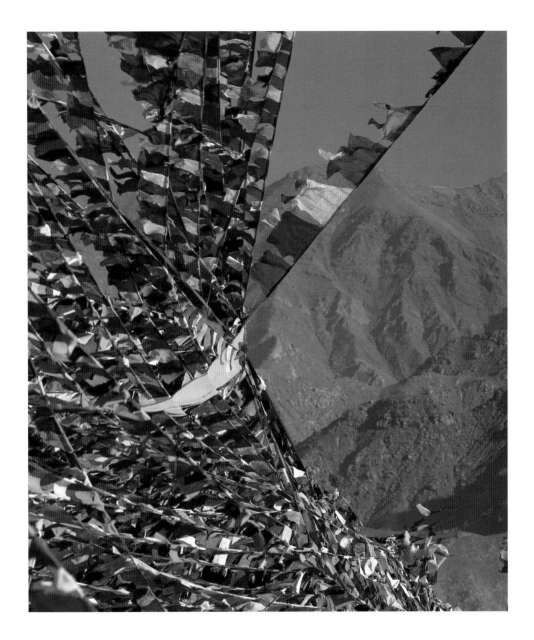

Left, New prayer
flags hung on
Bompori Hill, above
Lhasa, Tibet, as part
of Tibetan New Year
festivities.

less powerful compared to an instance where the person has
acted out all stages completely – with a strong motivation,
actual execution, and a sense of taking pleasure or satisfaction from the act committed. Similarly, there could be cases
where the individual may have a very weak motivation but
circumstances force him or her to actually commit the act. In
this case, although a negative act has been committed it
would be even less powerful than in our first example,
because a strong motivating force was not present. So
depending on the strength of the motivation, of the actual
act, and of the completion, the karma produced will have
corresponding degrees of intensity.

On the basis of these differences, the scriptures discuss four
types of karma: karma which is carried out but not accumulated, karma which is accumulated but not carried out,
karma where the act is both carried out and accumulated,
and karma where there is an absence of both accumulation
and the actual execution of the act. It is important to understand the significance of this point, and to appreciate that
since there are different stages to every act, karmic actions
themselves are composite, and their quality can be characterized as the cumulative result of each of their composing
factors.

Once you appreciate this, then whenever you have the
opportunity to engage in a positive action as a Dharma practitioner, it is important to ensure that at the initial stage your
positive motivation is very strong, and that you have a strong

intention to engage in the act. Then, while you are actually carrying out the act, you should ensure that you have given it your best, and you have put all your effort into making the action successful. Once the action is performed, it is important to ensure that you dedicate the positive karma that you have thereby created towards the well-being of all beings as well as your own attainment of enlightenment. If you can reinforce that dedication with an understanding of the ultimate nature of reality, it would be even more powerful.

Ideally, as Dharma practitioners, we should of course try to avoid engaging in any negative actions at all, but even if we do find ourselves in a situation where we are committing a non-virtuous action, it is important to make sure that at least our motivation is not strong and there is no strong emotion involved. Then, even while we are carrying out the action, if we have a strong pang of conscience, and a sense of regret or remorse, then of course the negative act will be very weak. Finally, the action should not be followed by any sense of satisfaction. We should not take pleasure in any negative action we have committed, but rather we should feel deep remorse and regret, and immediately afterwards we should purify the negativity, if possible. If we can do this, if we can live a way of life where we relate to our positive and negative

Above, Mandala in the roof of chorten at the site of the former western gate of Lhasa, Tibet.

Left, Pilgrims prostrating in front of the Jokhang Temple at dusk, Lhasa, Tibet.

actions in this way, then we will be able to follow the teachings on the law of karma much more effectively.

Although there are many different types of negative action, the Buddhist scriptures summarize them as the Ten Negative or Ten Non-virtuous Actions. There are three actions of body, four of speech, and three of mind. The three bodily negative actions are killing, stealing, and sexual misconduct; the four negative actions of speech are lying, engaging in divisive speech, using harsh words, and engaging in senseless gossip; and the three negative mental actions are covetousness, harbouring harmful thoughts and intentions, and holding wrong views. Ideally, a Dharma practitioner should live in such a way that he avoids all these negative actions if possible, and if not, then at least he should refrain from as many as he can. Leading a disciplined life and avoiding negative actions is what Buddhists understand as an ethical way of life.

Left, Shepherd at Yamdrok Lake, Tibet.

KARMA AND THE PERSON

How does a Buddhist practitioner actually go about trying to lead a moral life? A person's ultimate aspiration is to attain enlightenment, so one of his or her principal tasks is to gain victory over the kleshas. However, there is no way that a practitioner can directly combat negative emotions and thoughts at the initial stage, so the sensible way to proceed is simply

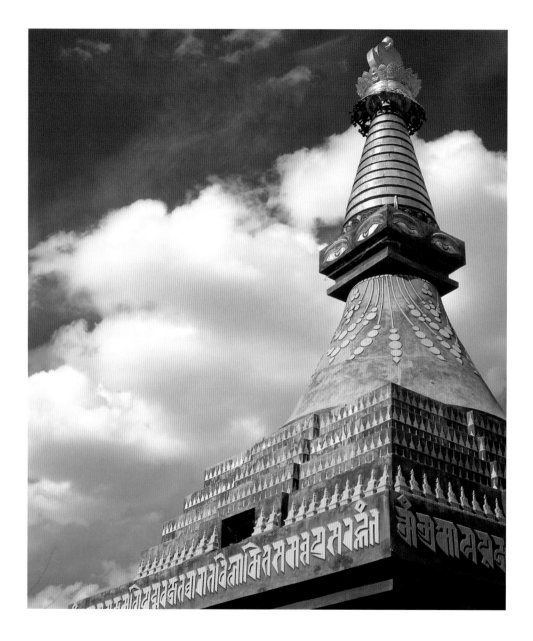

to find a way of containing the expression of the negative actions of our body, speech and mind. The first step, then, is to guard our body, speech and mind from engaging in negative actions so that we don't give in to the power and domination of our negative thoughts and emotions.

Left, Chorten at Samye Monastery, Tibet.

Once you have achieved this first stage, you can proceed to the second stage and tackle the root cause – the fundamental ignorance of which we spoke earlier. At this stage you are able to counteract the forces of the kleshas directly. Once you can do that, the third stage consists not simply of gaining victory over them, but also of rooting out all the propensities and imprints they have left within the psyche. This is why Aryadeva states in the *Four Hundred Verses on Madhyamaka* that a true spiritual aspirant must first overcome negative behaviour, in the middle phase must counter any grasping at self, and in the final stage should overcome all the views that bind us within the samsaric realm.[2]

As we have already seen, Buddhism explains how both the environment and the sentient beings living in that environment are produced as a result of fundamental ignorance, particularly the karma which arises from ignorance. However, we should not think that karma produces these things from out of nowhere. This is not the case. Karma is not like an eternal cause. We should realize that in order for karma to operate, and in order for it to have the potential to create its consequences, it must have a basis on which to do so. It follows that there exists a continuum of both the physical and the mental worlds. We can trace the continuum of the physical world to the beginning of a particular universe, and then we can even trace that "beginning" to empty space. Buddhism accepts the existence of what are known as "space particles" and asserts there is a stage of empty space in which the source of the material universe is in some sense contained. In the case of the mental world, we cannot say that the continuum of consciousness in sentient beings is a result of karma. Neither can we say that the unending process of the continuity of both matter and mind results from karma.

If this is the case, if the basic continuum is not produced by karma, then where does karma fit in? At what point does karma play a causal role in producing sentient beings and the natural environment in which they live? Perhaps we can say that there is a natural process in the world, and at a certain point when its evolution has reached a stage where it can affect the experiences of beings – giving rise to either painful experiences of suffering or joyful experiences of happiness – that is the point where karma enters the picture. After all, the karmic process only makes sense in relation to the experience of sentient beings.

So if we were to ask whether consciousness is produced by karma, or whether sentient beings are produced by karma, it seems the answer should be "no". But on the other hand, if we ask whether the human body and the human consciousness

Right, Khampa man outside Hezou Monastery, Eastern Tibet.

are products of karma, then the answer is "yes" because both result from virtuous actions. This is because, when we talk about the human body and human consciousness, we are referring to a state of existence which is directly related to the painful and pleasurable experiences of an individual. Finally, if we were to ask whether or not our natural instinct to seek happiness and overcome suffering is a product of karma, it seems the answer would again be "no".

KARMA AND THE NATURAL WORLD

Now when we turn to the evolution of the physical universe at large, we cannot say that the natural processes of cause and effect are a product of karma. The process of cause and effect in the natural world takes place regardless of karma. Nevertheless, karma would have a role to play in determining the form that the process takes, or the direction in which it leads.

Here we should mention that from the Buddhist analytical point of view, we distinguish two realms of enquiry. One realm we could call "natural", where only the natural process of causal laws operates, and the other is where certain properties emerge, contingent on these causal interactions. On account of this distinction we find that different avenues of reasoning are used when trying to understand the nature of the world or of reality.

For example, in Buddhist analysis we use what we call the

Four Principles. The first is the *Principle of Nature*: the fact that things exist, and that causes lead to effects. We could almost say that this principle implies an acceptance of natural laws. Then we have the *Principle of Efficacy*: this deals with the way things have the capacity to produce certain results according to their nature. The third is the *Principle of Dependence*: given the first two principles, we see there is a natural dependence between things and events, between causes and effects. On the basis of these three principles, Buddhist critical analysis applies various types of reasoning to broaden or deepen our understanding of the natural world. Therefore the fourth principle we accept is the *Principle of Valid Proof*: given this, that must be the case; and given that, this should be the case.

For a practicing Buddhist, it is important to appreciate these principles of the natural world, so that one is in a position to utilize that knowledge to live a life that is in accord with the principles of Dharma. We could therefore say that by living according to the Dharma we would be applying the Principle of Valid Proof, in terms of the way in which we avoid negative actions and enhance virtuous actions.

So, as 1 mentioned earlier, the

Left, Looking through decorated doorway to large prayer wheel spun by a monk at Labrang Monastery.

Below, Spinning prayer wheels in the Jokhang Temple, Lhasa, Tibet.

questions we now have to consider are: at what point in the causal process does karma come into the picture? and in what manner does karma interact with the process of the natural causal laws?

Perhaps we can refer to our own personal experience in order to answer these questions. Experience shows that certain actions we do in the morning, for example, will have a continuing effect even in the evening. The action will have created a certain state of mind. It will have had an impact upon our emotion and our sense of being so even though it was committed in the morning as an event that is finished, its effect still lingers on in our mind. I think the same principle operates with karma and its effects, even in the case of long-term karmic effects. This is how we understand that karma can create effects which are felt even a long time after the act was committed. According to the Buddhist explanation, of course, the impact of karma can be felt over successive lifetimes as well as in our present life.

At this point I feel that unless we complement the general explanation of the karmic process found in the Buddhist literature[3] with points from the Vajrayana literature, our understanding will not be complete. The Vajrayana explains that both the physical world and the bodies of living beings are composed of the five elements: earth, water, fire, wind, and space. Space here should be understood in terms of vacuum, of empty space, rather than as space in the technical sense of absence of obstruction. The Vajrayana literature discusses these in terms of external elements and internal elements, and shows how they are related to each other at a very profound level. Through understanding this relationship, our insight into the way karma affects the world is a much deeper one.

As we discussed earlier, the fact that consciousness exists is a natural fact. Consciousness exists; that is it. Similarly, the continuum of consciousness is also a natural principle: consciousness maintains its continuity. To this we must add that in Buddhism, there is an understanding that consciousness cannot arise from nowhere or without a cause; and, at the same time, that consciousness cannot be produced from matter. This is not to say that matter cannot affect consciousness. However, the nature of consciousness is sheer luminosity, mere experience; it is the primordial knowing faculty, and therefore it cannot be produced from matter whose nature is different. It follows that since consciousness cannot arise without a cause, and since it cannot arise from a material cause, it must come from a ceaseless continuum. It is on this premise that Buddhism accepts the existence of (beginningless) former lives.[4]

We have seen that the origin of suffering lies in both karma and ignorance, but actually ignorance is the principal origin.

KARMA AND THE EMOTIONS

There are differences in the way each school of Buddhism understands the nature of the kleshas, corresponding to their various interpretations of the doctrine of *anatman*, or no-soul theory. For example, certain states of mind, and certain thoughts and emotions which, according to the Madhyamaka-Svatantrika and Chittamatra schools, may be considered non-delusory, are seen as delusory from the point of view of the Madhyamaka-Prasangika school. This is a very complex point, of course, and would require a lot of study.

The most important thing for us to know is that afflictive emotion is our ultimate enemy and a source of suffering. Once it develops within our mind, it immediately destroys our peace of mind, and eventually destroys our health, and even our friendships with other people. All negative activities such as killing, bullying, cheating and so forth, stem from afflictive emotion. This, therefore, is our real enemy.

An external enemy may be harmful to you today, but tomorrow could become very helpful, whereas the inner enemy is consistently destructive. Moreover, wherever you live the inner enemy is always there with you, and that makes it very dangerous. In contrast, we can often keep an external enemy at some kind of distance. In 1959, for example, we escaped from Tibet since escape was a physical possibility; but in the case of this inner enemy, whether I am in Tibet, or

Above, Butter lamps in the Jokhang Temple, Lhasa, Tibet.

Left, Thangka painting of Shakyamuni Buddha, Tibet.

in the Potala, or in Dharamsala, or here in London, wherever I go it follows me. I think the inner enemy is even there in meditation; and even if I visualize a mandala, I may still find this enemy in its very center! So this is the main point we have to realize: the real destroyer of our happiness is always there within us.

So what can we do about it? If it is not possible to work on that enemy and to eliminate it, then I think we had better forget the spiritual path and rely on alcohol and sex and other such things to improve our lives! However, if there is a possibility of eliminating the inner enemy, then I think we should take the opportunity of having a human body, a human brain and a good human heart, and combine these strengths to reduce and ultimately uproot it. This is why human life is considered to be so precious according to the Buddhist teachings, for it alone enables a being to train and transform the mind, mainly by virtue of intelligence and reasoning.

Buddhists distinguish between two kinds of emotion. One type is without reason, and is just based on prejudice. Hatred is one of these. This sort of emotion will rely on superficial reasons, of course, such as "this person has hurt me terribly", but deep down, if you pursue that reasoning further, you find it does not go very far. Emotions without proper reason are what we call negative emotions. The other kind of emotion, which includes compassion and altruism, is emotion with reason because through deep investigation you can prove it is good,

Right, Three young monks in Ganden Monastery, Tibet.

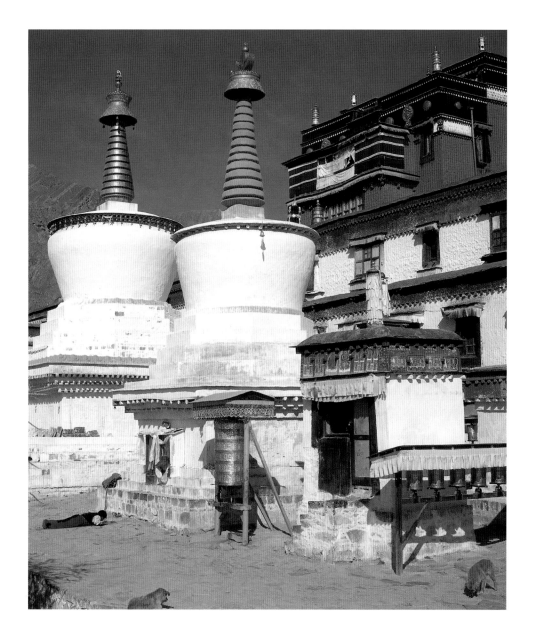

necessary and useful. Furthermore, although by nature it is a type of emotion, it is actually in accord with reason and intelligence. In fact, it is by combining our intelligence and emotion that we can change and transform our inner world.

So long as the inner enemy is there, and so long as we are under its control, there can be no permanent happiness. Understanding the need to defeat this enemy is true realization, and developing a keen desire to overcome it is the aspiration to seek freedom, technically called renunciation. Therefore this practice of analyzing our emotions and our inner world is very crucial.

The scriptures say that so far as the desire to overcome the first level of suffering is concerned, the "suffering of suffering", even animals have it naturally. And so far as the aspiration to free oneself from the second level of suffering is concerned, the "suffering of change", this is not something that is unique to the Buddhist path. Many ancient Indian non-Buddhist paths were similar, seeking inner tranquillity through samadhi. However, the genuine aspiration to seek complete liberation from samsara can only arise from a recognition of the third level of suffering, the "suffering of conditioning", where we realize that so long as we remain under the control of ignorance we will be subject to suffering, and there will be no room for lasting joy and happiness. It may be said that the recognition of this third level of suffering is unique to the Buddhist path.

Left, Woman prostrating in front of chortens beside Tashilumpo Monastery, Tibet.

THE TRUTH OF CESSATION

THE THIRD OF THE
FOUR NOBLE TRUTHS

The third Noble Truth is the Truth of Cessation. The key questions we must ask ourselves on this are the following: What is nirvana? What is *moksha* or liberation? What do we mean by *nirodha* or cessation? And is it really possible to attain cessation or not?

If we were to reply that we must accept that liberation is possible on the grounds that Buddha spoke of it in the scriptures, I don't think that is a satisfactory answer. It may be useful to reflect on a point that Aryadeva makes in his *Four Hundred Verses on the Middle Way.* He argues that when we talk about the ultimate nature of reality, or emptiness, we must realize that the understanding of emptiness is not something which requires reliance on scriptural authority. We can approach it through critical analysis and reasoning.

In Buddhism, we assert that one category of phenomena manifest to us and can be perceived directly, so there is no need for any logical proof of their existence. A second category of phenomena may not be obvious to us, but we can infer their existence through a process of reasoning. These are technically known as "slightly obscure phenomena". Emptiness belongs to this second category.[1]

Since we can infer the truth of emptiness, we must also accept that liberation can be inferred through the reasoning process too. As Nagarjuna says, a true understanding of liberation should be based on an understanding of emptiness, because liberation is nothing other than the total elimination, or total cessation, of delusion and suffering through

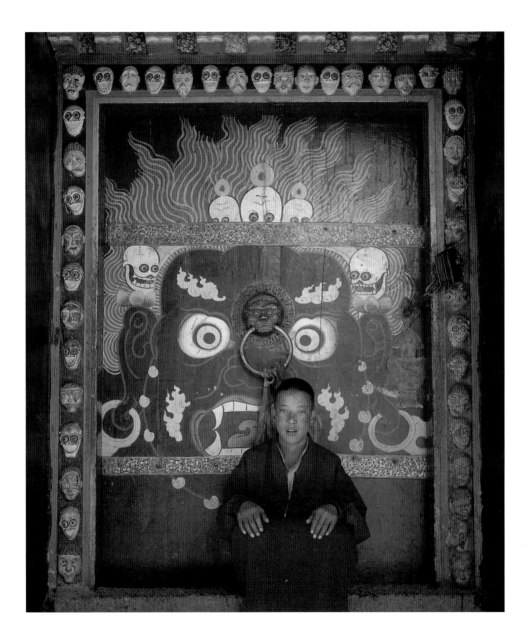

insight into emptiness. The concept of liberation is therefore very closely related to that of emptiness, and just as emptiness can be inferred, so can moksha.

On account of this intimate connection between emptiness and liberation in Buddhism, the passage in Maitreya's *Abhisamayalamkara* which deals with the third Noble Truth contains an extensive discussion of the 16 types of emptiness. The fact that liberation is an ultimate truth (and therefore related to emptiness) is explicitly discussed in Chandrakirti's writings as well. So it seems that our acceptance of liberation as a possibility is a function of how well we understand the concept of emptiness.

EMPTINESS

Four Interpretations of "No-self" or Emptiness

When we talk about emptiness in Buddhism, it is clear that we are referring to the absence of something, a form of negation. In the same way, the no-self theory is a form of negation. Why such insistence on categorical negation? Once again, let us pause for a while and consider our experience.

Let's imagine that I have a certain fear based on some kind of suspicion that there might be something threatening nearby. If the thought occurs to me that I may be mistaken, that

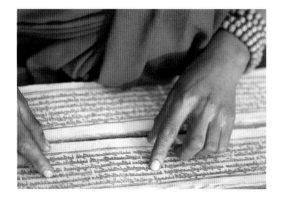

Above, Young
monk of Langmusi
Monastery reading
a prayer book,
Eastern Tibet.

Right, Monk
holding a mala.

it may be my projection, then although it will lessen my fear it will not completely dispel it. However, if instead 1 develop the thought that it is pure and utter illusion, that there isn't anything there at all and I'm just imagining it, and if my negation is that categorical, then of course it will have an immediate impact on dispelling my fear. The question is: if that is the case, what is actually being negated? What is empty of what?

According to the scriptures, emptiness in this example is an absence of the object of negation, which in this case is the object of our fearful apprehension. This does not explain things fully, however, so we have to go further and try to understand what the object of negation actually is. The key to this question really lies in the way we understand the meaning of atman (self) in the context of anatman (no-self). Depending upon one's philosophical interpretation of the Buddha's teaching on anatman, there will be differences in the way one identifies what is being negated here.

Buddhist literature expresses varying degrees of subtlety concerning the identity of the atman as an object of negation. For instance, on one level[2] the atman is identified as substantially real, as a soul that exists within each one of us,

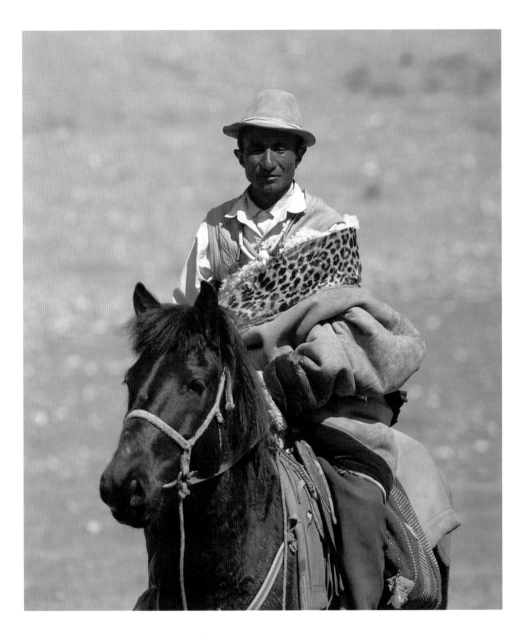

and so in this context anatman means the negation of a substantially real, autonomous agent or eternal soul.

Then we have the interpretation of the Chittamatra school, which understands fundamental ignorance not as the belief in a substantially real and eternal soul, but rather as the belief in the reality of the physical world. The Chittamatrins understand fundamental ignorance, then, as the (erroneous) belief in the duality of mind and matter, so the object to be negated with respect to anatman is precisely this belief.

Thirdly, there is the Madhyamaka-Svatantrika understanding of emptiness. According to this school, although things come into being as a result of causes and conditions, and although the status of things as existing is in one sense or another dependent on our perception, nevertheless there is a certain intrinsic reality to things and events. What is negated by this school is the assertion that objects exist independent of perception, and it is this that constitutes their understanding of emptiness.

From the point of view of the Madhyamaka-Prasangika school, however, that is not the final meaning of the Buddha's teaching on anatman. According to this view, so long as we have not deconstructed or dismantled the notion that things and events can have any type of intrinsic existence whatsoever, then we are still grasping at things as real, as though they enjoyed some kind of independent status. Therefore the Prasangika-Madhyamikas negate the intrinsic

Left, Horseman on the Sangke grasslands with leopard-skin coat, Eastern Tibet.

existence and identity of things and events, and claim that *this* is the true meaning of emptiness.

Despite these differences, what all four schools have in common is a concern to emphasize that while we are rightly engaged in counteracting our grasping at the self, it is important to ensure that our negation does not defy the reality of the conventional world, the world of lived experience. There is a shared understanding that causality and the operation of karma should not be negated in the process. It seems that the Madhyamaka-Prasangika approach is the most successful in this respect, in so far as it uses a form of analysis that allows a thorough and complete negation of atman, while at the same time ensuring that the world of dependent origination and of karma is not destroyed but, on the contrary, re-affirmed.

Left and above, Making a sand mandala at Samye Monastery, Tibet.

THE MIDDLE WAY

There is a very important passage[3] in Nagarjuna's *Fundamental Treatise on the Middle Way (Madhyamakamulakarika),* where he states: "That which is dependently originated, I call empty. And that is, in turn, dependently designated". The idea is that whatever is dependently originated is empty in the ultimate sense, and that what we designate, dependently, is nothing other than empty phenomena. The fact that things and events

are dependently designated implies that they are not non-existent, they are not mere nothingness. So when an understanding of dependent origination is combined with an understanding of emptiness, we find that this enables an individual to tread the Middle Way, so-called because it avoids the extremes of absolutism and nihilism.

So the Madhyamaka expression "dependently designated" has a deep significance. The first word, "dependently", implies that things and events come into being through dependence on other factors, which means that they do not possess independent, autonomous, or absolute existence. So this first point negates absolutism. The second word, "designated", implies that things and events are not mere nothingness, that they are not non-existent – that they do indeed exist. This part of the expression therefore ensures that the reality of the phenomenal world is not denied. As Buddhapalita states in his commentary on the *Fundamentals of the Middle Way*, if things and events have an independent existential status, and come into being without depending on other factors, then why are their designations dependent and interrelated?

In connection with this point, I have been told by various physicists that they are beginning to have problems in postulating an idea of reality that is in accordance with the quantum understanding of the physical world – even as a concept, reality is a problem. For me, this points to the difficulty of finding essences when we look into the essence of things.

Left, Nomadic yak herders, Spiti, Himachal Pradesh, India.

However, if we jump to the other extreme and say that everything is pure illusion and a mere projection of the mind, then we will be falling into the trap into which the Chittamatrins fell, namely the view of total mentalism. So if things do not possess intrinsic reality and yet, at the same time, if we are not happy with the conclusion that everything is a mere projection of the mind, what is the alternative? What is the middle way? The answer given by the Madhyamikas is that things and events arise purely as a result of the aggregation of many factors, and their conventional existence stems from the identity we impute to each aggregation.

As regards the exposition of the Buddhist doctrine of emptiness generally, we find there are many forms of reasoning presented in the literature which are designed to lead to an understanding of emptiness. Of all of these, the reasoning that is based on the understanding of dependent origination is considered to be the most effective. In order to develop the most profound understanding of the meaning of dependent origination, I think the works of Buddhapalita and Chandrakirti are crucial. Much of my own understanding and, naturally, most of the presentation I am making here, is based on Lama Tsongkhapa's exposition of these topics, which in turn is very much based on the reading of Nagarjuna by Chandrakirti and Buddhapalita, to the extent that Tsongkhapa substantiates almost every crucial point by referring to the commentaries of these two great masters.

When I study Nagarjuna's *Fundamentals of the Middle Way*, I combine the 23rd chapter dealing with the 12 links of dependent origination, with the 18th chapter on anatman. This latter chapter shows how it is the process of grasping at an eternal principle, or a substantially real soul, that binds us to unenlightened existence. It further shows how negating the principle of atman, and eliminating that grasping, lead to liberation. The main point is to underline how important it is to gain insight into emptiness.

❝ It is the process of grasping at an eternal principle, or a substantially real soul, that binds us to unenlightened existence. ❞

I then combine my study of these two chapters with that of the 24th, in which Nagarjuna anticipates a number of the objections which could be put forward by the realist schools of Buddhism. The core of their objections could be summarized in this way: if there is no intrinsic reality, and if there is no intrinsic existence and identity to things and events, then there is no-thing. It follows that there cannot be any Four Noble Truths; if there are no Four Noble Truths there are no

Left, Statues of Tsongkhapa in Manali, Himachal Pradesh, India.

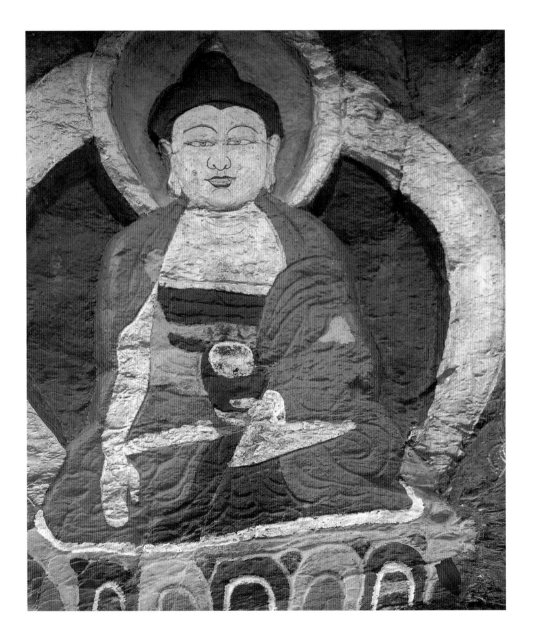

Three Jewels; if there are no Three Jewels there cannot be a Path to enlightenment. Nagarjuna responds by turning the realists' own criticism against them by saying that, on the contrary, if things do exist intrinsically then the consequences the realists attribute to his argument would apply to theirs. That is to say, if things are intrinsically real then the Four Noble Truths would not apply, nor could causes produce effects. So the central message of that chapter is to demonstrate that what Nagarjuna means by emptiness is not a mere nothingness, or a mere non-existence. Emptiness should be understood in terms of the interdependent nature of reality: it is by virtue of their dependent origination that things are devoid of independent existence.

Left, Rock painting beneath Chagpo Ri Hill, Lhasa, Tibet.

Lodrö Gyatso, a Tibetan master from Amdo, captured this point in a beautiful verse.[4] He said that emptiness in this context does not mean the absence of functionality. What does it mean then? It is the emptiness of real or absolute existence. Dependent origination does not entail intrinsic reality or intrinsic identity, but what it does entail is illusion-like, phenomenal reality. So when you understand the meaning of both emptiness and dependent origination, you can posit emptiness and appearance simultaneously, within one locus, without contradiction.

Furthermore, the same master added that all philosophical schools describe their own position as avoiding the extreme of absolutism by talking about some form of emptiness, and

avoiding the other extreme of nihilism by talking about the level of phenomenal reality. He pointed out, however, that it is only when you reverse the process that you overcome all forms of clinging: that is the Madhyamaka–Prasangika position, of course. From the point of view of Madhyamaka–Prasangika, then, it is through understanding appearance that a person is liberated from grasping onto absolutes, and it is by understanding the true meaning of emptiness that a person is freed from falling into nihilism.

Above, Mandala in the roof of the chorten at the site of the former western gate of Lhasa, Tibet.

Left, Detail of the Kumbum (large chorten) of Gyantse Monastery, Tibet.

THE MADHYAMAKA SCHOOLS

Earlier I spoke about there being two different understandings of emptiness even within the Madhyamaka school itself, and I outlined how the Madhyamaka-Svatantrika view differs from that of the Madhyamaka-Prasangika. The basis for accepting this difference comes from the writings of Bhavaviveka, one of the chief disciples of Nagarjuna, who subjects the Buddhist realist schools to very critical examination, and at the same time criticizes Buddhapalita's reading of Nagarjuna. Bhavaviveka's own position emerges through these two critiques. In essence, he maintains that although they deny absolute existence, they do accept some form of intrinsic and objective reality to things and events, which Madhyamaka-Prasangika masters like Chandrakirti totally reject. So although Chandrakirti, Buddhapalita and Bhavaviveka were all great disciples of Nagarjuna, there is a substantial difference in their respective understanding of Nagarjuna's philosophy of emptiness. It is on account of this difference that Tibetan Buddhist scholars distinguish two divisions within the Madhyamaka school, which they call Svatantrika and Prasangika.

Right, Monks debating at the Jokhang Temple, Lhasa, Tibet.

These two schools also differ in their methodology. The Madhyamaka-Prasangikas lay much greater emphasis on what is called the consequentialist style of reasoning. This resembles the *reductio ad absurdum* where you are not so much using reason to affirm something yourself, but rather you are concerned with showing the internal inconsistencies of your opponent's standpoint. In contrast, the Madhyamaka-Svatantrikas tend to use a syllogistic type of reasoning to establish their own positions.

Furthermore, there is another fundamental difference between Bhavaviveka and Chandrakirti which concerns the way our senses perceive material objects. For Bhavaviveka, it is valid to say that when a visual perception arises we see the appearance of an objective entity, because he accepts that things do possess a degree of objectivity which is then projected on to the perception. This is totally rejected by the Madhyamaka-Prasangika school of Chandrakirti. It is clear, therefore, that the central point of difference between the two Madhyamaka schools is whether or not one accepts any idea of intrinsicality.

APPLYING OUR UNDERSTANDING
OF EMPTINESS

Left, Prayer
flags leading to
Leh Monastery,
Ladakh, India.

The reason why it is so important to understand this subtle point is because of its implications for interpreting our own personal experience of life. When strong emotions arise in you, say attachment or anger, if you examine the experience of that emotion you will see that underlying it is an assumption that there is something objective and real out there which you are holding on to, and on to which you project desirable or undesirable qualities. According to the kind of qualities you project on to a thing or event, you feel either attracted to it or repulsed by it. So strong emotional responses in fact assume the existence of some form of objective reality.

However, if you realize that there is no intrinsic reality to things and events then, of course, this will automatically help you to understand that no matter how real and strong emotions may seem, they have no valid basis. Once you know that they are actually based on a fundamental misconception of reality, then the emotions themselves become untenable. On the other hand, if your understanding of emptiness is not thorough, in the sense that you have not succeeded in negating the notion of intrinsicality completely, then of course your attitude towards emotion will be somewhat ambivalent, and you may feel that there is some sense in which it is valid or justified.

When you have developed a certain understanding of

emptiness, albeit an intellectual one, you will have a new outlook on things and events which you can compare to your usual responses. You will notice how much we tend to project qualities on to the world. More especially, you will realize that most of our strong emotions arise from assuming the reality of something that is unreal. In this way you may be able to gain an experiential sense of the disparity between the way you perceive things and the way things really are. The moral that we can draw from all of this is that the strong emotions which afflict our mind arise from a fundamental state of confusion, which leads us to apprehend things as real and existing independently. In conclusion, we know that afflictive emotions and thoughts have no valid basis, neither in our experience, nor in reality, nor in reason.

Left, Pilgrim couple making offerings shortly before dawn on the hills above Ganden Monastery, Tibet.

" **Most of our strong emotions arise from assuming the reality of something that is unreal.** "

By contrast, your insight into the emptiness of things is not only grounded in reason but also in experience: it has valid support. In addition, your understanding of emptiness and your grasping at things as real are directly opposed to one other, so

one cancels the other out. Since they are opposing forces, and given that one has valid grounding whereas the other does not, the final conclusion we can draw is that the more we deepen our understanding of emptiness, and the greater the power of our insight becomes, the more we see through the deception of emotions, and consequently the weaker those emotions become. Indeed, we come to realize that strong afflictive emotions and thoughts, and their basis which is ignorance, can be weakened, while insight into emptiness can be enhanced.

LIBERATION

We have arrived at a point in our examination where we can conceivably accept that the power of delusions and of ignorance can be reduced, but the question remains as to whether it is at all possible to eliminate them completely and eradicate them from our minds. Some of the points in Maitreya's *Uttaratantra* may be very critical here. According to that text, our potential for knowledge is intrinsic to our consciousness and is an inherent, natural quality of our mind, whereas all those factors which afflict the mind are not an essential part of it. Mental afflictions are distinct from the essential nature of our mind, and are therefore called adventitious.

So when we talk about gaining the perfect wisdom of a buddha, we should not think that we need to create

Left, Preparing for the arrival of His Holiness the Dalai Lama at Kungri village in Spiti, Himachal Pradesh, India.

qualities in ourselves that are not there already, and acquire them from somewhere outside of us. Rather, we should see perfect buddha wisdom as a potential that is being realized. The defilements of the mind hamper the natural expression of that potential which is inherent in our consciousness. It is as if the capacity for unobstructed knowledge is there in our mind, but the defilements obscure and hinder it from being fully developed and expressed. However, once our understanding of the mind is informed by the idea that the essential nature of mind is pure luminosity and mere experience, or the sheer capacity to know, we can then conceive of the possibility of eliminating these afflictions completely.

To sum up, in this chapter we have followed the conceptual approach to the question of whether or not it is actually possible to attain liberation.

Finally, if we accept that liberation is possible, how exactly is it to be understood? In the scriptures, liberation is characterized in terms of four features. The first feature describes it as the true cessation of the continuum of afflictions. According to the second feature, liberation is true peace, the state of total tranquillity where the individual has attained complete freedom from all defilements of the mind. It is described in the third feature as totally satisfying, because one has reached ultimate satisfaction. Fourthly, it is described as definite emergence, in the sense that one has definitely emerged from the process of unenlightened existence.

THE TRUTH
OF THE PATH

THE FOURTH OF THE FOUR
NOBLE TRUTHS

Previous photograph,
Man spinning
prayer wheels while
walking around
Sakya Monastery,
Tibet.

Left, Leh
Monastery,
Ladakh, India.

If we accept that liberation is an achievable goal, how is it possible to achieve it? This question brings us to the fourth Noble Truth, which deals with the true path.

According to the Madhyamaka explanation, the true path should be understood in terms of developing a direct intuitive realization of emptiness. This is because the intuitive realization of emptiness leads directly to the attainment of cessation. However, in order to have such a realization one must have a basis in single-pointed meditation, since this is what leads to an experiential knowledge of emptiness. The point at which an individual attains that experiential knowledge[1] is said to be the beginning of what is called the Path of Connection or Path of Preparation, and the point at which he gains direct intuitive realization of emptiness is called the Path of Seeing.

The experiential knowledge of emptiness must in turn be based on an intellectual understanding of emptiness, developed through inference. Indeed, without that, it is impossible to attain a meditatively-based experience of emptiness. That initial stage of developing intellectual understanding is part of what is known as the Path of Accumulation. The threshold of this path is the point where the practitioner develops a genuine aspiration to attain liberation – and this we consider to be the very beginning of the Buddhist Path.

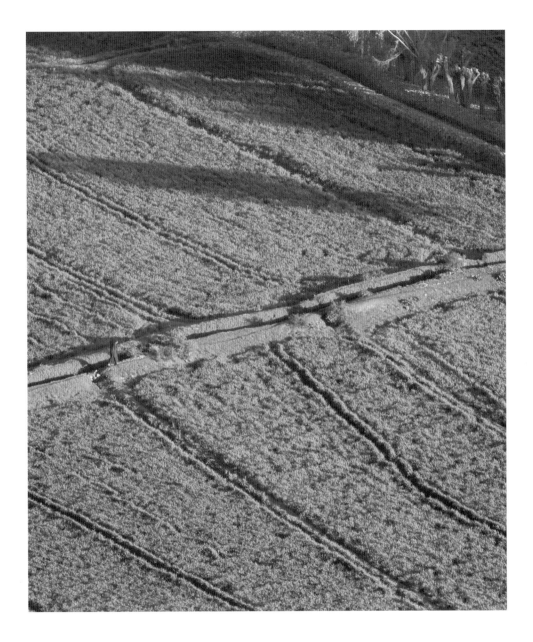

THE SHRAVAKAYANA PATH

Even before we embark upon the Path,[2] a great deal of preparation is necessary. To begin with, the most important practice is that of the three higher trainings: the trainings in morality (Skt. shila), concentration or meditation (Skt. samadhi), and wisdom or insight (Skt. prajña). The scriptures generally describe the transition from one stage to another in terms of a meditator's experience. It is important to understand, therefore, that the actual path on which the individual travels is that of his or her progressively deepening knowledge and realization of emptiness, technically known as the wisdom aspect of the path. Moreover, the wisdom that realizes emptiness must be developed within the context of the union of the single-pointedness of mind and penetrative insight, known as the union of shamatha and vipashyana.

In order to experience a union of these two, we have to develop shamatha first, for only this will enable us to channel our energy and concentration. Training in shamatha is therefore key. For it to be successful two factors must be present, namely the application of mindfulness and the application of mental alertness. These two capacities themselves will only develop successfully if our single-pointedness of mind is based on an ethically sound life, in which we apply discipline both to our attitude and to our way of life. This, of course, underlines the fundamental importance of morality. So now we can see

Above, Silhouette of the Jokhang Temple before dawn, Lhasa, Tibet.

Left, Monk walking through the fields beside Samye Monastery at dawn, Tibet.

how the three trainings are connected to each other.

All of these practices are common to both the Shravakayana and the Mahayana.

THE MAHAYANA PATH

We must now look at another important aspect of Buddhism, namely the way that the entire teaching of Buddha is founded on compassion. Compassion is the very foundation of the Dharma. The practice of enhancing our good heart and developing an altruistic mind is aimed at deepening our understanding of compassion, and invigorating the compassionate potential that exists within us. It is on the basis of profound compassion that we develop the altruistic aspiration to seek enlightenment for the benefit of all.

Traditionally this is called the generation of bodhichitta. What is bodhichitta? In Maitreya's *Abhisamayalamkara* bodhichitta is described as having two motivating factors: the first is genuine compassion towards all beings, and the second is recognition of the need to attain full enlightenment in order to fulfil the welfare of others. Indeed, to develop the altruistic mind of bodhichitta, it is not enough to have mere compassion. Bodhichitta must be based on a compassion which carries a sense of responsibility so that you are willing to take upon yourself the task of helping others.

Right, Young monk in warm robes at Monlam prayer festival after Tibetan New Year at the Jokhang Temple, Lhasa, Tibet.

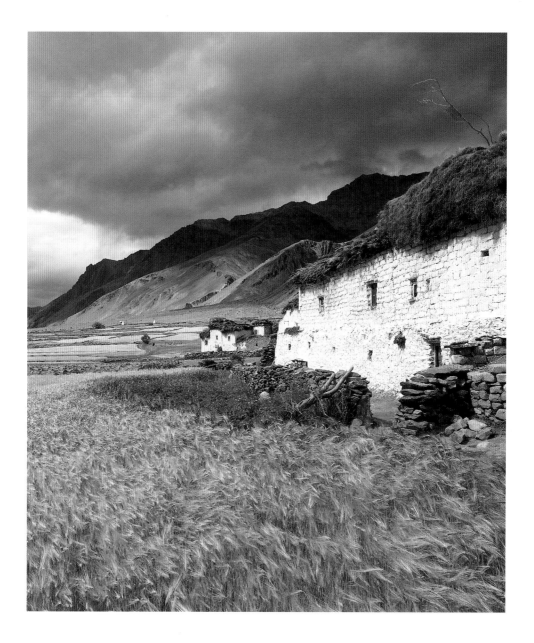

This sense of responsibility will only arise if you have generated a spontaneous, genuine compassion which extends to all sentient beings without exception. This is universal compassion. It is called *mahakaruna* or "great compassion" to distinguish it from ordinary compassion which is limited. However, this itself will not arise unless you have genuine insight into the nature of suffering, both your own suffering and that of others. You recognize your state as being one of suffering, then you will also feel a genuine empathy and connection with others. So far as gaining insight into the nature of suffering is concerned, reflection on the first Noble Truth, the Truth of Suffering, will assist you in deepening your insight.

For an altruistic practitioner, it is important to realize that attaining liberation for oneself alone is not enough. Not only is it individualistic, but even from the point of view of one's own path to perfection, it is not a state of full awakening.

It is therefore crucial to nurture our natural empathy and our sense of closeness with others. One of the methods described in the Buddhist scriptures for doing this is to imagine that all beings are your mothers, or someone else who is dear to you. You awaken the compassion you naturally feel for your mother or someone dear, and extend it to all other beings. In this way you develop a natural and spontaneous empathy. However, empathy cannot arise if your emotions towards others fluctuate due to the fact that you view some as enemies and others as friends. That discrimination has to be overcome

Left, Barley fields beside houses near Phuktal Monastery, Zanskar, India.

Left, Monks
going to perform an
offering ceremony
(puja) at Labrang
Monastery,
Eastern Tibet.

first, and for this the practice of equanimity is fundamental.

A different method is presented by Shantideva in *The Guide to the Bodhisattva's Way of Life (Bodhicharyavatara)*. He explains a way of cultivating genuine empathy by considering others as equal to oneself. For example, just as you personally wish to be happy and overcome suffering, others too have a similar desire, and just as you have the right to achieve this, so do they. With that sense of equality you reverse your self-centred perspective, putting yourself in others' shoes and relating to them as if they were dearer to you than you are to yourself.

According to the Tibetan tradition, these two different methods are combined and then meditated upon. Once you have gained even a simulated experience of the altruistic mind as a result of your reflection and meditation, then the custom is to stabilize and reinforce it by participating in a ceremony where you explicitly generate bodhichitta. This should then be followed by a keen desire to engage in the activities of a bodhisattva. According to tradition, the practitioner formally takes the vows of a bodhisattva at that point. The bodhisattva ideal, or the activities of a bodhisattva, are summed up in the Three Precepts: the first is the precept of refraining from negative actions; the second is the precept of deliberately engaging in virtuous actions; and the third is the precept of helping others.

From the point of view of how causal practices lead to a resultant state, bodhisattva practices are also sometimes

described in terms of the two accumulations: the accumulations of merit and wisdom. The two accumulations come together in the union of method and wisdom and, in the Buddhist path, should never be separated.

THE VAJRAYANA PATH

The profundity and sophistication of Tantra or Vajrayana stem from the practice of unifying method and wisdom. To put it very briefly, one of the unique features of the union of method and wisdom in the Vajrayana teachings is that the practitioner first subjects his or her perception of self and the world to an understanding of emptiness, and dissolves everything into emptiness. That cognition of emptiness is then visualized (imaginatively, of course, at the beginning) as the perfect form of a meditational deity. Next, you reflect on the non-substantial or empty nature of that deity. So within one instance of cognition, both method and wisdom are present and complete: there is visualization of a deity and at the same time an understanding of the empty nature of that deity.

Within the Vajrayana tradition there are four principal classes of tantra according to the Gelug, Sakya and Kagyu schools; these are Kriya tantra, Carya tantra, Yoga tantra, and Highest Yoga tantra (Anuttarayogatantra). The first two classes do not involve taking Vajrayana vows; it is in the Yoga tantra and

Above, Chung-chen bird statue on the roof of the Jhokang Temple, Lhasa, Tibet.

Left, Pilgrims throwing "wind-horses" into the air on Bompori Hill as part of the Tibetan New Year festivities, Lhasa, Tibet.

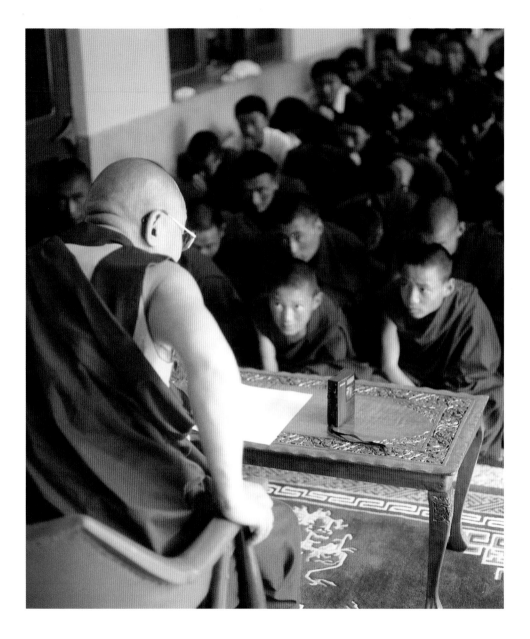

Highest Yoga tantra that tantric vows are taken. The Highest Yoga tantra also has meditative practices which use various physiological elements, such as visualizing the energy channels of the body, the energies that flow within the channels, the "subtle drops", and so on. In all of these various types of meditation the key is always the aspiration of bodhichitta and insight into emptiness. Without these two factors none of them would even be considered to be Buddhist practices.

However, in some very reliable and authentic texts belonging to Yoga tantra, it is said that the Vajrayana path can also be based on the understanding of emptiness held by the Chittamatra school, not necessarily on that of the Madhyamaka. Despite this, I feel that if tantric practice is to be comprehensive, and if one is to attain full realization of the tantric path, an insight into emptiness based on the Madhyamaka is actually crucial.

ADVICE ON FOLLOWING
THE BUDDHIST PATH

There are three pieces of advice I would like to share with you.

The first is to say that unless you are able to establish a firm grounding in the basic practices of the Buddha Dharma, such as those I have outlined, then even the supposedly profound practices of the Vajrayana will have no effect. The point is that for a practicing Buddhist, it is really vital to develop an understanding of the Four Noble Truths, and to meditate upon them. Meditation should therefore be an essential part of your practice, and include both shamatha and vipashyana.

Another important factor is your determination. You should not imagine that all these developments can take place within a few days or a few years; they may even take several aeons, so determination is evidently vital. If you consider yourself a Buddhist and want to really practice Buddha Dharma, then right from the start you must make up your mind to do so until the end, regardless of whether it takes millions or billions of aeons. After all, what is the meaning of our life? In itself, there is no intrinsic meaning. However, if we use life in a positive way, then even the days and the months and the aeons can become meaningful. On the other hand, if you just fritter your life away aimlessly then even one day feels too long. You will find that once you have a firm determination and a clear objective, then time is not important.

As Shantideva writes in this beautiful prayer:

66 **For as long as space exists
And sentient beings endure,
May I too remain,
To dispel the misery of the world.**[3] 99

His words really convey a certain understanding to me, and they are so inspiring.

My final point is that the more impatient you are, and the more you want the way that is quickest, cheapest or best, the more likely you are to obtain a poor result. So I suggest this is the wrong approach.

Left, Monk performing circumambulation of a chorten beside Ganden Monastery, Tibet.

CONCLUSION

If I were to essentialize my talk, I would say that if your understanding of the Four Noble Truths arises from deep reflections such as these, then you will gain a profound admiration for the Dharma, which is the true Refuge, and you will also develop a conviction in the possibility of actualizing the Dharma within yourself. On the basis of such a conviction you will be able to develop genuine devotion in the Buddha, the master who showed you the path, and you will also have a deep respect for the Sangha members who are your spiritual companions on the path.

If your understanding of the Three Jewels is based on a realization of the Four Noble Truths that is as profound as this, then whenever you think of Buddha, Dharma, and Sangha, they will come alive for you with renewed freshness. This is what is meant by Going for Refuge.

In fact, to summarize even more succinctly, the whole of

the explanation I have given here is to show what is meant by Going for Refuge in the Three Jewels.

Although my own practice is very poor, very poor indeed, and although I recite mantras and visualize certain mandalas, even so the main emphasis of my daily practice is the Four Noble Truths and bodhichitta. These two practices I feel are of real practical benefit. Sometimes I think that visualizing deities can almost be like a way of deceiving oneself. In my view we must pursue practice step-by-step, with patience and determination. If you practice in this way, then after a year or after a decade you will notice at least some improvement in yourself, and when you see that, it brings a new encouragement to continue. However, we must realize that change is not at all easy.

So now you have read these teachings on the Four Noble Truths, if you consider you are a Buddhist then please put them into practice. They should not remain merely on an intellectual level. Practice and teaching must be part of our life. The same applies, of course, to practitioners and believers of other faiths, such as Christians, Muslims or Jews: whatever your faith, if you accept that faith then it must become part of your life. It is not sufficient to attend church on Sunday and join your hands together in prayer for a few moments, if the rest of your behavior remains the same. Whether or not you are physically in a church or a cathedral, I think the teaching of your own religion must be in your

Above, His
Holiness the
Dalai Lama at
the Royal Albert
Hall, London
in May 1999.

heart. That's very important. Only then will you have an experience of it that is of real value, otherwise it is simply a piece of knowledge in your head and when you are faced with problems in life it won't be of any help.

Once the teaching is part of your life, whenever you have a real problem it gives you inner strength. Also, when you grow old, or have an incurable illness, and when death finally comes, then your practice truly gives you some kind of inner guarantee. After all, death is part of life; there is nothing strange about it; sooner or later we all have to pass through that gate. At that time, whether or not there is a life after, it is very valuable to have peace of mind. How can we achieve peace of mind at such a moment? It is possible only if we have some experience in ourselves that will provide inner strength, because no-one else can provide this for us – no deities, no gurus, and no friends. This is why the Buddha says you must be your own master.

GLOSSARY

Abhidharmakosha (Treasury of Knowledge) by Vasubandhu. English translation (from a French translation) by Leo M. Pruden, *Abhidharmakoshabhashyam*, Berkeley, California, Asian Humanities Press, 1991.

Abhidharmasamuchchaya – see Compendium of Knowledge

Arhat (Tib. dgra bcom pa) – to become an Arhat is the final goal of the Shravakayana. It is a form of nirvana, beyond rebirth, but falls short of buddhahood. The Tibetan word literally means "one who has subdued the enemies", i.e. negative emotions.

Aryadeva – a disciple of Nagarjuna and author of many important commentaries.

Asanga – great Indian master, half-brother of Vasubandhu, who composed important Mahayana works inspired by Maitreya. He is especially known as a proponent of the Chittamatra school. Circa 4th century.

Bhavaviveka – also known as Bhavya, the key figure in the development of Svatantrika-Madhyamaka.

Bodhicharyavatara – see Guide to the Bodhisattva's Way of Life.

Bodhisattva – a being who has decided to bring all beings to enlightenment and who is practicing the Bodhisattva path of the Mahayana.

Buddhapalita – circa 4th century Indian master, founder of Prasangika-Madhyamaka.

Chandrakirti – circa 3–4th century master, the greatest figure in the Prasangika-Madhyamaka school.

Chatuhshatakashastrakarika – see Four Hundred Verses on the Middle Way

Clear Words (abbreviated Skt. title: Prasannapada; full title: Mulamadhyamakavrttiprasannapada) – a commentary by Chandrakirti on Nagarjuna's Mulamadhyamikakarika. English translation of selected chapters in M. Sprung, 'Lucid Exposition of the Middle Way'.

Commentary on the Compendium of Valid Cognition (Pramanavarttikakarika) by Dharma-kirti. No English translation.

Compendium of Knowledge (Abhidharmasa-muchchaya) by Asanga. French translation by Walpola Rahula, **Le Compendium de la Super- Doctrine**

(Philosophie d'Asanga), Paris, Ecole Française d'Extrême-Orient, 1971.

Dharmakirti – famous Buddhist master of the 7th century.

Emptiness (Skt. shunyata) – the absence of true existence in all phenomena.

Enlightenment (Skt. bodhi) – purification of all obscurations and realization of all qualities.

Four Hundred Verses on the Middle Way (Chatuhshatakashastrakarika) by Aryadeva. English translations by K. Lang, **Aryadeva's Chatuhshataka: On the Bodhisattva's Cultivation of Merit and Knowledge**, Indiske Studier, Vol. VII, Copenhagen, Akademish Forlag, 1986; and Geshe Sonam Rinchen and Ruth Sonam, **Yogic Deeds of Bodhisattvas: Gyelstap on Aryadeva's Four Hundred**, Ithaca, Snow Lion, 1994.

Fundamentals of the Middle Way (Mulamadhyamikakarika) – a seminal text by Nagarjuna. English translation by F. Streng, **Emptiness: A Study in Religious Meaning**, Nashville and New York, Abingdon Press, 1967. See also K. Inada, **Nagarjuna: A Translation of his Mulamadhyamikakarika**, Tokyo, Hokuseido Press, 1970.

Guide to the Bodhisattva's Way of Life (Bodhicharyavatara) by Shantideva. English translations include **A Guide to the Bodhisattva's Way of Life** by Stephen Batchelor, Dharamsala, Library of Tibetan Works and Archives, 1979; and **The Way of the Bodhisattra**, translated by the Padmakara Translation Group, Shambhala, Boston, 1997.

Liberation (skt. moksha) – freedom from samsara, either as an arhat or as a buddha. **Madhyamaka** – literally "the middle way". The highest of the four main Buddhist schools of philosophy. First expounded by Nagarjuna and considered to be the basis of Vajrayana. The Middle Way means not holding to any extreme views, especially those of eternalism and nihilism.

Mahayana – literally "the Great Vehicle", the vehicle of bodhisattvas. It is great because it aims at full buddhahood for the sake of all beings.

Maitreya – the Buddha to come, the fifth in this present cosmic age. Many Mahayana teachings were inspired by Maitreya.

Mandala – the universe with the palace of a deity in the centre, as described in the Tantric practice of visualization.

Mantra – manifestation of supreme enlightenment in the form of sound. Syllables used in Tantric visualization practices to invoke the wisdom deities.

Mulamadhyamikakarika – see Fundamentals of the Middle Way

Nagarjuna – Indian master of 1st–2nd century CE who expounded the teachings of Madhyamaka, and composed numerous philosophical treatises.

Path of accumulation – the first of the five paths according to Mahayana. On this path one accumulates the causes that will make it possible to proceed towards enlightenment.

Path of connection – the second of the five paths according to Mahayana. On this path one connects oneself to, or prepares oneself for, seeing the two kinds of absence of self.

Path of seeing – the third of the five paths according to Mahayana. It is called this because one really sees the two kinds of absence of self, that of the individual and that of phenomena.

Pramanavarttikakarika – see Commentary on the Compendium of Valid Cognition

Prasannapada – see Clear Words

Samsara – the cycle of unenlightened existence in which one is endlessly propelled by negative emotions and karma from one state of rebirth to another. The root of samsara is ignorance.

Shamatha – "calm abiding". The meditative practice of calming the mind in order to rest free from the disturbance of thought.

Shantideva – great Indian poet and master of the 7th century C.E.

Shravaka – follower of the root vehicle of Buddhism (Shravakayana) whose goal is to attain liberation from the suffering of samsara as an arhat. Unlike bodhisattvas, shravakas do not aspire to attain enlightenment for the sake of all beings.

Shravakayana – the vehicle of the hearers or listeners, based on the teachings of the Four Noble Truths.

Sutra – the teachings of both the Shravakayana and the Mahayana.

Uttaratantra – the full Sanskrit title is Mahayana-uttaratantrashastra (Supreme Continuum of the Mahayana). This text is ascribed to Maitreya. English translations from the Sanskrit by E. Obermiller, **Sublime Science of the Great Vehicle to Salvation in Acta Orientalia** 9 (1931), pp. 81–306; and J. Takasaki, **A Study on the Ratnagotravibhaga**, Rome, ISMEO, 1966. English translation from the Tibetan by Ken and Katia Holmes, The Changeless Nature, Dumfriesshire, Karma Drubgyud Darjay Ling, 1985.

Vajrayana – literally "the diamond vehicle", also known as Tantrayana.

Vasubandhu – great Indian master, brother of Asanga, who composed classic philosophical works on the Sarvastivada, Sautrantika and Chittamatra doctrines.

Vipashyana – clear insight meditation.

NOTES

INTRODUCTION

1.   Dependent origination, or dependent arising, are translations of the Sanskrit *pratitya samutpada*. It is the natural law that all phenomena arise "dependent upon" their own causes "in connection with" their individual conditions. Everything arises exclusively due to and dependent upon the coincidence of causes and conditions without which they cannot possibly appear.

2.   A buddha is literally someone who is awakened (from Sanskrit *bodhi*, awake) so buddhahood is the awakened state.

3.   "Cessation" is a technical term meaning 'the complete cessation of suffering'. Samsara refers to the cycle of suffering, and the cessation of that cycle is commonly identified as nirvana.

4.   See *Majjhima Nikaya I*, p. 190–191, Pali Text Society. See also the *Pratityamutpada Sutra*.

CHAPTER ONE

1.   The Changeless Nature, translation of the *Uttaratantra* by Ken and Katia Holmes, Karma Drubgyud Darjay Ling, UK, 1985. Page 135. The *Uttaratantra* is also known as the *Ratnagotravibhaga*.

2.   The Twelve Links of Dependent Origination form the twelve-fold cycle of causal connections which binds beings to samsaric existence and thus perpetuates suffering. These Links are depicted around the famous Buddhist Wheel of Life, which illustrates the six realms of samsara and their various causes. The Links are, going clockwise around the Wheel: ignorance, volition or karmic formations, consciousness, name and form, the six bases of consciousness, contact, feeling, desire, attachment, becoming, birth, and old age and death. See *The Meaning of Life from a Buddhist Perspective* by His Holiness the Dalai Lama, translated and edited by Jeffrey Hopkins, Wisdom Publications, 1992.

CHAPTER TWO

1.   For a detailed treatment of Buddhist cosmology in English, see *Myriad Worlds* by Jamgon Kongtrul, Snow Lion, 1995.

2.   The human world is part of the Desire Realm. The Formless Realm is more subtle than the Form Realm, which in turn is more subtle than the Desire Realm.

3.   The early teachings of Buddhism are divided into the Vinaya, or code of discipline, the Sutras, or discourses of the Buddha, and the Abhidharma which is the commentarial and philosophical literature composed by Buddhist masters. Two complete corpuses of Abhidharma literature have survived to the present day: that of the Theravada school, in Pali, and that of the Sarvastivada school, in Sanskrit. Only the Sarvastivadin Abhidharma was taught in Tibet. The chief reference on cosmology is Chapter Three of Vasubandhu's *Abhidharmakosha,* translated into English by Leo Pruden, Asian Humanities Press, Berkeley California, 1991.

4.   Three Aspects of the Path, verse 7. See Robert Thurman's *Life and Teachings of Tsongkhapa,* Library of Tibetan Works and Archives, Dharamsala, India, 1982.

5.   According to Tibetan Buddhism there are six realms in samsara, each dominated by a particular mental poison. They are: the hell realms (anger), the animal realm (ignorance), the realm of pretas or hungry ghosts (miserliness), the human realm (desire), the demi-god or Asura realm (jealousy), and the god realm (pride).

6.   This statement can be found in *Majjhima Nikaya I* (p. 262, Pali Text Society) and *Majjhima III* (p. 43, Pali Text Society) and *Samyutta Nikaya II* (p. 28, Pali Text Society).

7.   Buddhist psychology bases the perception process on six sense faculties: sight, hearing, smell, taste, touch and thought. Each faculty relates to a sense organ (eye, ear, nose, tongue, body, mind) and to a consciousness which functions specifically with that organ. There are thus six sense consciousnesses, the sixth one being the mental consciousness.

CHAPTER THREE

1.   The term "karma' comes from the Sanskrit word "karman", meaning 'action'. It has three main meanings in Indian philosophy. The first is karma as ritual action, namely the sacrifice, in the early Vedas and Mimamsa philosophy. The second is karma as a particular category of human action, namely defiled and limited action, which we find in Samkhya Yoga, Advaita, the Bhagavad Gita and Buddhism. And the third meaning refers to karma not as an action but as a theory of action, in particular the theory of action as causal determinant. It is to this third meaning that the Dalai Lama refers here.

2.   *Chatuhshatakashastrakarika*, chapter 8, verse 15.

3.   See in particular the third and fourth chapters in Vasubandhu's *Abhidharmakosha.*

4.   See a fuller discussion of this topic by His Holiness the Dalai Lama in dialogue with David Bohm in *Dialogues with Scientists and Sages: The Search for Unity,* edited by Renée Weber (Routledge and Kegan Paul, London, 1986).

CHAPTER FOUR

1.   The third category of phenomena are "very obscure phenomena", which are beyond ordinary direct perception and logical inference. Generally, they can only be established on the basis of another's testimony or through scriptural authority.

2.   This view is held in particular by the Shravakayana schools, especially the Vaibhasikas or Sarvastivadins, and the Sautrantikas.

3.   Chapter XXIV, verse 18.

4.   His Holiness is referring to a text known as *The Interwoven Praise* (sPal mar bstod pa), which is a commentary in verse on Tsongkhapa's famous *Praise to the Buddha for his teachings on Dependent Origination* (rTen 'brel bstod pa). Lodrö Gyatso was a late nineteenth century Gelug master from Amdo and was more widely known as Chone Lama Rinpoche.

CHAPTER FIVE

1.   See the *Dasabhumika Sutra* for an explanation of the stages of the bodhisattva path.

2.   In the Indian tradition, the Buddhist path was generally presented as the Noble Eightfold Path, which is composed of: right view, right intention, right speech, right action, right livelihood, right effort, right meditation, and right concentration. The Tibetan tradition also describes the Buddhist path in terms of the Five Paths, which are the path of accumulation, the path of connection, the path of seeing, the path of meditation, and the path of no more learning. Within this framework, the Noble Eightfold Path would be included in the path of meditation.

3.   The Bodhicharyavatara by Shantideva, X.55.